Depth Charge!

View of the stern and wake of a minelayer with depth charges on deck.

Depth Charge!

Mines, Depth Charges and Underwater Weapons, 1914–1945

Chris Henry

Pen & Sword
MILITARY

First published in Great Britain in 2005 by
Pen & Sword Military
an imprint of
Pen & Sword Books Ltd
47 Church Street
Barnsley
South Yorkshire
S70 2AS

ISBN 1-84415-174-3

Typeset in 11/13pt Plantin by Mac Style Ltd, Scarborough, N. Yorkshire
Printed and bound in England by CPI UK

Pen & Sword Books Ltd incorporates the Imprints of Pen & Sword Aviation,
Pen & Sword Maritime, Pen & Sword Military, Wharncliffe Local History, Pen
& Sword Select, Pen and Sword Military Classics and Leo Cooper.

For a complete list of Pen & Sword titles, please contact
Pen & Sword Books Limited
47 Church Street, Barnsley, South Yorkshire, S70 2AS, England
E-mail: enquiries@pen-and-sword.co.uk
Website: www.pen-and-sword.co.uk

Contents

Acknowledgements

Writing a book on a very technical subject is never an easy task. Without the aid of illustrations, it would be very difficult indeed to explain many of the concepts gathered here. I have several people to thank in helping me with this project: in particular, George Malcolmson of the Royal Navy Submarine Museum, who helped me with research and also with his own fabulous collection of early images, many of which grace this book.

I would also like to thank my colleague Ian Proctor, who carried out a lot of preliminary research at the National Archives, and Mike 'Hockers' Hockin for inspiration and listening to my long diatribes about Herbert Taylor. Thanks also go to Alan Pilledge, who worked at West Leigh Cottage, and to his friend David Clark for their willingness to answer my e-mails with endlessly tedious questions. They were both eye-witnesses to some of the Second World War activities described in this book. Without their help, I would not have been able to follow through some of my leads nor get some of the more interesting titbits published here. Finally, I must mention members of the Naval Historical Branch of the MoD – Captain Chris Page, Katherine Tildesley, Ian McKenzie and Jenny Wraight – who helped me just as they were moving their archive from London to Portsmouth.

Many of the photographs reproduced here have come from the collection of Explosion, the Museum of Naval Firepower in Gosport, which was originally the Royal Naval Armament Depot of Priddy's Hard. As Head of Collections at the museum, I have been privileged to work with this fine collection of artefacts. Amongst this treasure trove were the personal papers of Herbert John Taylor, which inspired me to write this book. The photographs are mainly glass-plate negatives – some were used for training at HMS *Vernon* and others came from Vosper Thorneycroft at Woolston – and none has been published before, to my knowledge.

Chris Henry
Gosport, Hants.
May 2005

Chapter One
Introduction

In my youth, in the late 1960s, it was quite a common thing for the senior male in a household to have a garden shed to take refuge in when he needed a place to be alone. These sheds were often places of mystery and could conceal anything from a huge model-train set to pigeons and even rare orchids. One such man that I knew was always making small engineering pieces on a miniature lathe and I was fascinated by the way he could create an intricate engineering masterpiece from bits of old rod and bar. In those days there were many hobby magazines that detailed how to build steam engines or model boats. I particularly remember one called *Model Engineering*, an amazing magazine that showed all kinds of techniques and ideas for recreational engineering. This individual engineering creativity still exists in Britain, but from the 1930s to the 1950s it was at its height. It may be that amateur creative genius found an outlet in this sort of activity, but for others it was their lifeblood.

Mechanical engineering was a thriving industry in Britain, particularly influential in the Victorian and Edwardian eras. Inevitably, one of its chief applications was in warfare. Along with mechanical engineering, new uses were being found for electrical power, uses which were making themselves felt in the armed services – so much so that, by the First World War, it had become an essential element of naval technology. Mines were often detonated by electrical systems, whereas naval guns used electrical systems for signalling or firing. By the end of that war, the reliance on mechanical and electrical engineering was all-encompassing.

People who had that rare ability to think out and plan such mechanisms were people to be coveted. In the later 1930s and the 1940s, the scientific battle had become just as important as the front-line combat going on all over the world. This book of necessity moves between inventions of the two world wars and concentrates on the development of depth charges and mines. It is not meant to be an exhaustive account of every weapon, but rather an explanation of some of the weapons, linked to the stories of some of the men who invented them.

A shallow-firing depth charge exploding during tests.

It is likely that I have omitted some personal stories, if only for lack of space. If anyone feels aggrieved that I have not covered all the significant personalities in the world of explosives, then I apologize in advance. It is worth noting that many of the people involved in technical developments in the First World War were again employed in the Second. So many weapons were being developed between 1915 and 1945 that not just naval personnel but all sorts of people were drawn into military projects.

This book is about the relationship between civilian inventors, often with nothing more than the garden-shed facilities mentioned above, and the Admiralty. It deals with the invention of underwater weapons and the personalities who designed and built them, tested them and finally used them. Dwight Messimer, the American historian of underwater weapons, has examined the political effects of the appearance of the submarine and so in this work I have tried to analyze the imperatives – financial, and in some cases political – that underlay the production of new underwater weapons. The role of the civilian inventor and his expectations of financial recompense are major issues in this work. I hope to demonstrate that the Admiralty worked on various levels – the creativity and skill of men in workshops and obscure departments, no less than the efforts of senior officers – to produce a series of viable anti-submarine weapons.

All wars fought from the middle of the nineteenth century onwards have not only been a struggle of armies or navies on the battlefield but also a struggle of rival technologies. The invention of a new weapon or defensive system had to be met by finding a countermeasure. It could be argued that this has always been the case. In the Middle Ages, the crossbow gave its users the advantage because of its greater range. When gunpowder was invented, its powerful explosive effect was quickly put to use. This see-saw effect was easily recognizable in the naval world in the specification of battleships between 1860

The Royal Navy's obsession, the big-gun ship.

and 1880, when more powerful guns firing armour-piercing shells were countered by thicker and tougher armour plate.

By the twentieth century the whole pace of technical change had stepped up a gear and the influence of technological change was widely felt. This book aims to deal with the scientific and technical efforts used to combat submarines and surface ships, and it should stated here that it is not a history of the torpedo. That subject has been dealt with admirably by authors such as Edwin Gray and Geoff Kirby, who (I must say) are far better equipped to deal with the subject than myself. I have attempted to look at key developments in the advancement of underwater explosive weapons, in the light of the activities of several hitherto unknown designers and engineers. These are shadowy people of whom we only know little, and that mostly through their activities in the two world wars. The submarine was one of the greatest naval inventions of the nineteenth century, but at first its advent was considered of little import to navies around the world. The ability to creep up unseen and attack a valuable warship with a relatively inexpensive torpedo was obviously a major advantage to the weaker nation that had the weapon, but this was not obvious to the powers that be at the early stages of the First World War, for example. Submarines were used to some effect in the American Civil War, and the French and Spanish experimented with them in the last two decades of the nineteenth century. It was the American inventor John Phillip Holland who really started the ball rolling by designing a viable underwater attack vessel that could be used to attack shipping with locomotive torpedoes – meaning a self-

British naval service mine on board. George Malcolmson Collection

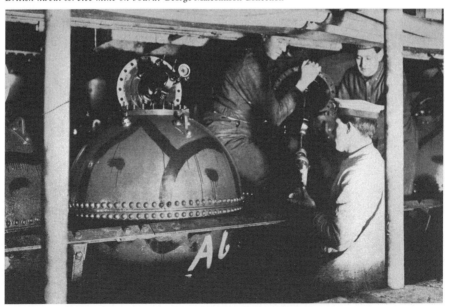

propelled weapon that could be aimed and fired on a pre-determined course. The Holland VI was a 74-ton submarine that could travel for 1,000 miles on the surface and on 12 October 1900 the United States purchased their first. The Royal Navy was not long to follow and Vickers built five Holland boats under licence at Barrow-in-Furness between 1901 and 1903.

The main thrust of tactical thinking in the late nineteenth and early twentieth centuries was based upon the need to destroy the enemy surface fleet. The submarine was new and untried. Many explosive devices were constructed to destroy the surface ship. Mines were an example of this type of weapon and a sort of naval mine was used as early as the eighteenth century. David Bushnell (1742–1824), inventor of the manned submersible *Turtle*, was responsible for creating a sort of barrel mine, which was going to be used against British warships during the American revolution. Between Christmas 1777 and January 1778 an attempt was made to attack British frigates in the Delaware River, using Bushnell's barrel mines, but without success.

These early devices were as simple as a floating barrel of gunpowder: the device was fired by an actuating lever, which in turn fired a flintlock and exploded the main charge. This type of device was intended to float down a river and explode when it contacted a ship at anchor. This technique obviously left a lot to be desired and random drifting explosive charges needed to be controlled in some way so that there was at least some way of ensuring a chance of success.

At the beginning of the nineteenth century, the most notable designer was the American Robert Fulton. The Royal Navy discussed Fulton's ideas with

U-boats in port about 1908.

him, resulting in an attack on the French fleet at Boulogne in October 1804. Fulton called his explosive devices 'torpedoes', but we would probably call them mines. As with many weapon designers, he had also offered his ideas to the French. The Crimean War saw some use of explosive mines, and the Russians had some success with them, but the First World War was the first war in which large quantities of mines were developed and deployed, and submarines came into their own. In the years before 1914, planning for all contingencies, Britain's intention was to attack French submarines with those of the Royal Navy. It soon became clear that they would be far more useful than this limited role allowed.

The Royal Navy first officially considered anti-submarine measures in 1903. On 29 December, the Commander-in-Chief Home Fleet was to organize manoeuvres that would allow the navy to evaluate tactical methods of destroying submarines.[1] In 1911, the submarine *Holland No. 2* was attacked with primitive depth charges to see what the effect would be. From these experiments it became clear that an underwater explosive charge would be a serious threat to a submarine. There were two problems: first to detect the submarine and then to get the charge within range. It was considered that, if successful, even if the boat were not damaged, the effect on morale would be enough to put the boat out of the fight.

On the eve of the First World War, one of the few establishments developing and testing naval weapons was HMS *Vernon* in Portsmouth. The Admiralty began to set up research organizations from scratch and one modern historian has demonstrated that this harnessing of scientists and engineers was not an

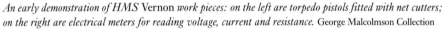

An early demonstration of HMS Vernon *work pieces: on the left are torpedo pistols fitted with net cutters; on the right are electrical meters for reading voltage, current and resistance.* George Malcolmson Collection

easy task.[2] A bewildering variety of committees and boards sprang up to explore inventions and their use in the war at sea. These organizations produced a stream of inventive proposals to develop weapons that would outwit the Germans and give Britain the technological edge. Two powerful factors in Edwardian naval organization over rode the need to find an anti-submarine weapon at the earliest opportunity. They were the predominant idea that the surface battle fleet was the most important element in any navy, and the predominant individuals who controlled the most important elements in naval tactical thinking. Throughout the First World War, the German and British navies considered the destruction of the opposition's surface fleet as one of the most important elements in their naval strategy; and it would be difficult to exaggerate the Edwardian navy's reliance on the actions of individual officers to carry out its policies.

By the end of the First World War, this was all beginning to change. The need for scientists and engineers was beginning to be recognized, partly because the submarine had inflicted massive losses on British shipping. The difficulties in trying to counter the submarine had been immense, and the only way to overcome the problem was to change tactics and introduce new and more lethal weapons. A new kind of naval officer began to emerge, one mainly concerned with the difficulties of physics rather than morale. Those men who began work in the Mining School and HMS *Vernon* were typical of these new officers.

Underwater weapons were problematic because they had to rely on a guidance system. On land, a gun could be aimed by an integral sighting system and fired at the target, normally using the eyes of an observer to give feedback through a telephone or radio link. At sea, naval gunnery relied on good optics to achieve a hit on the target. Under the sea, such systems were not possible and the use of sound location was essential. The sound locator – or Hydrophone, as it became known – was an essential part of the weapon system, all the elements of which had to be developed and co-ordinated within a short time. The fundamental difficulty was that science was mainly a civilian, theoretical enterprise rather than a military, practical one. In order to benefit from the most wide-ranging analysis of scientific problems, the navy had to rely on civilians for much of the experimental work. To get the best out of them presented problems of organization as well as motivation, problems which would be most difficult to overcome.

There were, however, people with a natural ability to create mechanical and electrical devices that speeded up the development of weapon systems, people who used pragmatic analysis, rather than pure theory, to make things work. There was always a tension between the navy's need to co-ordinate and implement the ideas of a group of inventive minds and for the individuals' need to be allowed a degree of freedom. It simply came down to this: individual or group effort? Human beings seldom do things in isolation; they are social animals who achieve goals by co-operation. Nevertheless there are certain individuals that are able to influence and guide projects so that their insight becomes the main force behind the development of new ideas and techniques. This book deals with some of these individuals and it gives an insight into the dynamic operating between groups of individuals within the navy.

The First World War saw the first sustained campaign waged by underwater vessels. The superiority of the British Grand Fleet over the German High Seas Fleet was not demonstrated, as the Royal Navy expected it would be, at the Battle of Jutland. The Royal Navy were able to bottle up the German fleet in harbour, but they could not destroy it: the Germans still had 'a fleet in being', to quote the Mahanian phrase. Although the High Seas Fleet was forced to stay in port after the battle, it remained a threat. The Germans returned to the submarine blockade in the last two years of the war and this proved to be the most logical choice, since the surface fleet could not seriously challenge the Royal Navy. The allies had to divert vast resources to limit their shipping losses.

At first the Royal Navy considered the use of submarines to be un-gentlemanly, but such officers as Percy Scott, the great gunnery reformer, and Admiral of the Fleet Jackie Fisher were well aware of the potential revolution submarines could cause – 'potential' because their effectiveness was compromised by the legal requirements of the Hague conventions. The submarine was considered a legitimate warship and as such was subject to International Law. If an attack was made, non-combatants had to be cared for and this completely lost the element of surprise, the main weapon of the submarine. This polite form of warfare was soon discarded, however, in favour of something far more vicious and effective.

Although the Germans had only thirty-five submarines in 1914, they issued the British with a wake-up call when the submarine U-9 sank the cruisers *Aboukir*, *Cressy* and *Hogue* on 22 September that year. There was also a tension between the political requirements of the German Government and the fear of provoking the United States into entering the war on the side of the allies. This became ever more likely when the unrestricted submarine campaign claimed American vessels. German U-boats were principally concerned with sinking Royal Naval vessels in the period between 1914 and early 1915, when they accounted for at least six large capital ships. It was not until 4 February 1915 that Germany declared unrestricted warfare on shipping around Britain. It actually started on 17 February. Fortunately, this campaign did not last longer than six months.

As is well known, the attack of U-20 on the liner *Lusitania* near Queenstown on 7 May 1915 brought the Americans shouting to the German Cabinet, and Kaiser Wilhelm had to stop attacks on passenger liners. Even with the kaiser's intervention, the U-boat commanders were difficult to control and other merchant ships were lost. The first campaign had not brought Britain to her knees, since she was able to build 2,000,000 tons of shipping to replace 900,000 tons lost. In contrast, the Germans had lost fifteen U-boats, but constructed only ten new ones.[3]

German propaganda showing U-1 and U-12 before the First World War. George Malcolmson Collection

It was not until 1917 that the prospect of unrestricted warfare surfaced again. This time the British blockade of the German coast meant that German food supplies were becoming severely limited. Once again the Germans turned to the U-boat to break the British will to make war. The cross-channel steamer *Sussex* was torpedoed and sunk on 24 March 1916 and the Americans made their strongest protest shortly afterwards. But the U-boat command was left in limbo for a further nine months until unrestricted warfare began again on 1 February 1917. Accordingly the Americans entered the war in April 1917, but this did not stop the German campaign, which continued until the end of the conflict. This time it was a different story and after Jutland one can say that most of the effort of the Royal Navy and the United States Navy was concentrated on countering U-boats or their cargoes, by means of mines and anti-submarine vessels.

According to a report to the Chief of US Naval Operations, it was considered that:

> most of the German submarines and especially the large ones after clearing the minefields off the German coast head directly for Fair Island between the Orkneys and the Shetland Islands and do not hesitate to pass through to the Atlantic. The British have found it wholly impracticable to net this passage. The submarines usually make a landfall at St. Kilda west of the Hebrides and thence down to the vicinity of Fastnet and the Scillys. They are usually out twenty days, eight of which are required for passage to and fro.[4]

Submarines continued to occupy the minds of naval commanders until the end of the war. It could be said that they were dealt with in two ways: offensively and defensively. Taking the latter strategy first, the obvious answer was the convoy, but this was not an obvious solution at the time. This book deals with the other anti-submarine strategy and the offensive measures taken in both world wars. In this case the most powerful weapon was the explosive charge, whether dropped overboard or propelled by a gun.

So what were the principal weapons that could be used against a submarine at the beginning of The First World War? At that time there were few viable anti-submarine weapons. The two obvious ones were ramming and gunfire. Ramming was the age-old tactic of physically hitting the submarine with your own ship. It might have occurred to the reader that this was likely to cause some damage to the attacking vessel and, yes, this was usually the case, but there are many instances of attacking vessels utterly wrecking the submarine victim without much damage to themselves. In other words, the risk was known but tolerated. In 1914 at least two German submarines, U-15 and U-18, were rammed and sunk, the former by HMS *Birmingham* and the latter by the destroyer HMS *Gary* off Scapa Flow.[5] Ramming sometimes also claimed the

The favoured method of disposing of a submarine at the beginning of the First World War was to ram the enemy. The damage sustained can be seen here on HMS Roxborough. George Malcolmson Collection

attacking vessel and HMS *Fairy* foundered on 31 May 1918 after ramming the U-boat UC-75 in the North Sea.

Gunfire continued to be effective in attacking a submarine, if the boat was on the surface and so detectable. After experiences in the Sea of Marmora, British submarines relied on the 12-pounder gun or the 3-inch of 20cwt gun[6] as a deck weapon. Sometimes more guns were fitted, two 4-inch guns in the case of British L class boats, whereas the Germans relied on an 88mm or 105mm gun, depending on the class. Submarines did attack other submarines with gunfire, but normally it was surface ships that did the damage. If we take a small coastal submarine such as the UC class, whose overall length was about 162ft, the majority of the target presented to a ship, even broadside-on, was the conning tower. Coupled with the unstabilized gun platform and the need for a submarine crew to get on deck to fire their gun, it is a wonder that any submarines were sunk by gunfire at all. Yet they were. The Germans lost twenty-three to gunfire alone.[7]

The Royal Navy also used heavily armed merchant ships as decoys, called Q-ships, to get close to submarines and damage them by gunfire. Even so, once the submarine had slipped beneath the waves it was safe from gunfire attack, except for the early moments of its dive. As it was, an attack from a submarine that used its gun was also a terrifying experience. Take the *Malachite*, for example. This cargo boat was four days out from Liverpool on 23 November 1914. At 15.45, when the ship was near the French coast, about an hour away from Le Havre, the crew spotted a submarine approaching, which fired a shot

Torpedo nets were the main defence against the torpedo throughout the first World War. Their deployment was complex, hardly suited to rapid evasion of the weapon. Manoeuvring was the most successful way of evading a torpedo hit.

The navy were always keen to show the public their new weapons. This mock-up of a minelayer was intended for a Navy Day pageant. George Malcolmson Collection

across the vessel's bows. The *Malachite* hove to and waited for the submarine. Under the shadow of the submarine's deck gun, the German submariners interrogated the crew. The U-boat commander gave the crew of the *Malachite* ten minutes to leave their ship. They then proceeded to fire at the vessel until enough holes were made in her hull to begin sinking her. It took the submarine about another hour to fill the ship full of holes, but she did not sink until the next day. The crew rowed themselves to Le Havre after an ordeal of three and a half hours.[8] This demonstrates how German submarines operated at the beginning of hostilities, with heavy reliance on the gun as the main offensive weapon, even though the vessel was designed to use torpedoes primarily.

There were two other means of attack: the mine and the torpedo. The term 'torpedo' can be confusing: what is normally referred to is the automobile torpedo, which was gyro-stabilized and perfected by the Bolton engineer Robert Whitehead in the last quarter of the nineteenth century, and developed further by the Royal Navy. Such a torpedo could be aimed and set to run on a course decided by the operator, without the need for further guidance once the gyroscope was set. But very few submarines were sunk by torpedoes in the early part of the war and we can disregard them until later. It was mines that proved their greatest threat, but British mines were unreliable and few.

Mines have been in existence since the Crimean War and the American Civil War. Some would say that they existed under different names even earlier than

The sinking of HMS Amphion *on 8 August 1914.* George Malcolmson Collection

that. During the nineteenth century they tended to be observed mines; in other words, they consisted of an explosive charge, in a container connected to an electrical system or mechanical device, that could be exploded by an observer at the correct time. By the First World War, the whole concept of mining had gained much more significance. The mine could be used as an offensive or defensive weapon. It could be laid at the mouths of channels to protect against invasion or it could seal off an enemy port if laid secretly.

HORN OF TYPES II, III AND IV GERMAN NAVAL MINE.

SHOWING THE DESIGN OF HORN FOUND ON THE TOP OF THE MINE.

*On the right is shown an attachment whose function is referred to in the text. On the left is shown a closing screw **A** which is inserted when the attachment is not in use.*

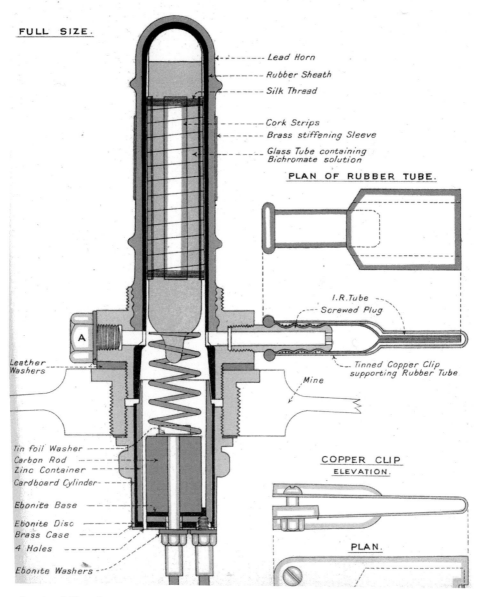

FULL SIZE.

Lead Horn

Rubber Sheath

Silk Thread

Cork Strips

Brass stiffening Sleeve

Glass Tube containing Bichromate solution

PLAN OF RUBBER TUBE.

I.R.Tube

Screwed Plug

A

Leather Washers

Tinned Copper Clip supporting Rubber Tube

Mine

Tin foil Washer

Carbon Rod

Zinc Container

Cardboard Cylinder

COPPER CLIP

ELEVATION.

Ebonite Base

Ebonite Disc

Brass Case

4 Holes

PLAN.

Ebonite Washers

A sectioned Hertz horn.

An interesting example of this occurred when the minelayer *Koenigen Louise* was despatched to lay mines off Lowestoft in August 1914. She was intercepted by a group of destroyers and the cruiser *Amphion*, which had been sweeping the Dutch coast. The *Koenigen Louise* was sunk by the cruiser but, in a supreme irony, the *Amphion* headed back to Britain only to be sunk herself on the minefield laid by the *Koenigen Louise*, killing the German prisoners-of-war who had laid them.

During the First World War, mines destroyed between forty-eight and fifty-five U-boats, some of which were sunk by their own mines. This was the biggest single cause of U-boats being lost during the war.[9] The mine was normally a metal case containing a large amount of explosive, typically between 100lb and 500lb. This charge needed to be set off by a mechanical or electrical device. In the First World War, mines were almost always exploded by contact with the target ship (hence the term 'contact mine') and many mines of this type had projections called 'horns' fitted to the case. One type of horn – known as the Hertz horn, after its inventor – consisted of a lead sheath around a glass phial full of an electrolyte. When the horn was hit by the ship, the lead sheath deformed, crushed the phial and released the electrolyte, which then completed an electromagnetic circuit exploding the mine.

How was a mine laid? The mine went into the water attached to a sinker – a sort of anchor that rested on the sea-bed. As the mine and sinker began their descent together, the sinker released (on its own line) a plummet, which fell faster than the mine and sinker. When the plummet hit the sea-bed, it stopped the line being paid out to the mine and this fixed the length of cable on which the mine floated, somewhere below the surface. The sinker filled with water, sank to the bottom and anchored the mine. This was known as an automatic mine. Sinkers were expected to be robust as they might be laid in heavy weather and there could be a 30ft drop from the minelaying sponsons of a ship. When the mine and sinker entered the water, the mine might be underneath and would not right itself on its descent; and it might be forced into violent motion by the currents and waves. This is why a tank was required when testing, so that different conditions could be imitated.

Apart from mines, other weapons were tried: explosive sweeps, nets, decoys and other strange devices. The towed sweep was probably the best attempt at blowing up submarines by explosives. The only devices in use at the beginning of the war were the single sweep and the modified sweep. The single sweep consisted of a solid metal 'kite' containing 100lb of explosive, towed by an electric armoured cable behind a ship and operated by an electric impulse. The 'kite' kept the device under water. By 1916, the view of HMS *Vernon* was that 'such a sweep is now considered to be comparatively valueless and incapable of further useful development'.[10]

The second type of towed apparatus, the 'modified sweep', was a vertically looped electric cable, again kept under water by a kite. The upper part of the loop consisted of a series of floats, while the lower part held a number of 100lb explosive charges. Each charge had a striker on it so, if one of the charges was set off, the whole line exploded. The sweep could also be detonated from the mother ship by electrical impulse. Some of the destroyers originally designed to use torpedoes were equipped with the modified sweep, but the quantity of explosive used was a serious hazard. It was thought that a torpedo boat destroyer with a total of 600lb of explosive on deck was very vulnerable – if not to enemy attack, then certainly to accidents. The equipment was also extremely cumbersome. The explosives, floats and extra laying-gear meant that a large area of the ship's deck had to be cleared to lay out the gear ready for use. They took time to deploy and this made it difficult to catch a submarine.

It might be worth mentioning probably the most ridiculous weapon produced for anti-submarine work. The lance bomb was an explosive charge on something that looked like a broom handle. It contained 7lb of amatol and was meant to be whirled around the head and thrown at the hull or conning tower of the enemy submarine. No known instance has been recorded of one even being used, still less with success.

The difficulty of deploying these devices and their limited use meant that many captains reverted to tried and tested methods of attacking submarines, namely the ram and the gun. In October 1914, the C-in-C Grand Fleet wrote to the Admiralty, pointing out that ramming was being resorted to for lack of a good weapon.[11] It was recognized that an explosive charge that could operate at varying depths was what was needed.

Chapter Two

Herbert Taylor and the Experimental Mining School at HMS *Vernon*

On 5 December 1945, W W Davis, Director of the Department of Torpedoes and Mines, wrote to Herbert Taylor, a civilian working for the navy, and summed up his contribution to the development of underwater weapons in the First and Second World Wars:

> You have served with us since 1915. You have been associated with the development of the depth charge, the depth-charge pistol, the principal of which still hold the field, chariots, X-craft, demolitions and many other miscellaneous weapons many of which have been and are in use in the Royal Navy. I know it will be a great source of satisfaction to you to know how valuable and efficient these weapons, with which you have been closely associated, have proved to be in service.[1]

A strange thing about the two world wars is that we often know a great deal about the weapons and technological advances in the Royal Navy's arsenal, but we know very little about the people that created the weapons. We all know names such as Barnes Wallis and Hiram Maxim, but who has heard of Herbert Taylor or Alban L Gwynne? The letter quoted above was high praise indeed for a man who had started off his life working on motor cars in Wandsworth, London. At the time this letter was written, Herbert Taylor was seventy years old. Over the years he became something of a well-known figure in the area of weapons development and had received accolades from his very small group of admirers. As an inventor he had clearly dedicated his life to finding new and unusual ways of overcoming physical problems. The London *Star* reported: 'Whenever Mrs. Herbert Taylor thinks of something that she would like to have done about the house she merely mentions it to her husband. And it is as good as done.'[2]

Herbert J Taylor, MBE, Hon. MIAE, was born at Claygate in Surrey on 9 September 1876 and retired from a long naval engineering career at

H J Taylor MBE.

Portsmouth on 22 December 1945. The tribute accorded to him by the Director of Torpedoes and Mines glosses over the fact that Taylor never seems to have been recognized officially by the authorities. He was paid a handsome sum from the Admiralty for his inventions, but he was never promoted above Engineer Grade One. Why this is remains a mystery and it may have something to do with his personality, the rigid hierarchy within the navy at the time, or a combination of these factors.

According to sources at the Museum of Naval Firepower in Gosport, Taylor had had a brilliant career at school. He had exhibited his mechanical engineering skills and was so gifted that he was recognized early as something more than a competent engineer. In the first half of the twentieth century it was common for young men to start engineering apprenticeships, which could last up to seven years. Taylor was apprenticed as an engineer with Messrs Spencers at Melksham in Wiltshire. After completing his apprenticeship, he set out as a journeyman until the advent of the motor car age. About 1898 he set himself up in business at a small engineering works at Wandsworth, where he revealed skill and ingenuity. He was appointed Instructor in motor engineering at Battersea Polytechnic; his pupils included many students from universities up and down the country.

In 1914, Taylor was concerned that submarines were a menace to British shipping. Many enthusiastic amateurs bombarded the Admiralty with ideas on how to combat submarines. Taylor set to work on an idea that was to become one of the simplest yet most efficient ways of operating an explosive charge under water. He had worked out that the increase in pressure as an object descends into deep water could be used to automatically fire an explosive charge at depth. Taylor devised a device known as the 'pistol': it was a hydrostatically operated detonator. It was basically a brass-and-steel mechanism about 2ft long, to be inserted into an explosive. It consisted of three main elements: the firing gear, normally a spring-operated striker designed to hit a detonator, the depth-setting gear, normally hydrostatically operated, and the safety gear.

Following his invention of the depth-charge pistol, he was asked in June 1915 to develop it and he joined the Admiralty's Experimental Mining School at HMS *Vernon*. The depth-charge pistol was quickly accepted for service, and

The Experimental Mining Department mechanical staff in 1917. A youthful Herbert Taylor is seated in the centre of the front row.

Taylor was then able to take a prominent part in the design of mine units, several of which, in certain basic aspects, have remained with little change until the present day. Taylor also had the distinction of being one of the pioneer motorists in the country: he began to drive in 1897. It was therefore fitting that the Institution of Automobile Engineers – now subsumed into the Institute of Mechanical Engineers – elected him to honorary life membership in 1941. This man therefore was to have a profound effect on the history of British underwater weapons. Why these weapons were so desperately needed requires more explanation.

On the eve of the First World War, the Royal Navy was really not prepared for the submarine. The first serious attempt to organize technology for the naval war came from the Anti-Submarine Committee in 1910. From then until war broke out, this was where most anti-submarine experiments were co-ordinated. In 1916 the Royal Navy integrated the Anti-Submarine Committee with the Operations Intelligence Division to form the Anti-Submarine Division. The Torpedo School at HMS *Vernon* in Portsmouth was one of the main experimental establishments. According to their yearly reports, much technical know-how was discussed and new experiments were considered, but much of their work was in the development of torpedo and mine warfare, rather than controlled scientific research.

There were three influential agencies responsible for developing anti-submarine technology. They were the Anti-Submarine Committee, the Director of Torpedoes and Mines, and the Director of Naval Ordnance. It is

HMS Vernon *as she was before the First World War, with HMS* Marlborough *nearest the camera. The three ships housed the whole of the torpedo and mining effort of the navy until the operation was moved ashore in 1917.*

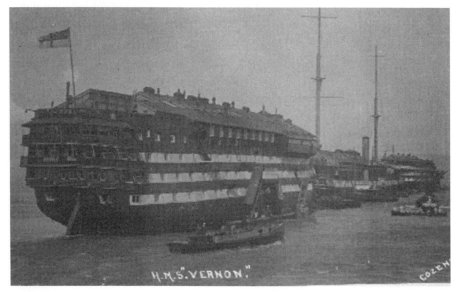

mainly with the Directorate of Torpedoes and Mines that this book is concerned. In the same way as there was a school of torpedoes, there was also a much smaller Mining School, which will be critical to our story. The Director of Torpedoes and Mines funded four different departments during the First World War: HMS *Vernon*, the Mining School, the Signal and Wireless Schools and the Paravane Department.

The link between civilian scientific research and naval demand eventually became the realm of the Board of Invention and Research, headed by none other than Admiral of the Fleet Lord Fisher from July 1915. When ideas were found, the board was meant to direct them to the correct naval department so they could be fully exploited. Many of the ideas discussed in this book were passed to HMS *Vernon*. Early in 1917 there were fundamental changes in the organizations that were part of the Naval Ordnance Department. The Torpedo Department was removed and placed under the control of the Director of Torpedoes and Mines, Rear-Admiral Fitzherbert. He had two assistants, one for torpedoes and one for mines. Jellicoe was a firm believer in expansion of the mining wing and he decided to give it more staff and more independence.

As part of a similar reorganization, the Admiralty created the post of Admiralty Controller, to oversee all naval shipbuilding and armament production, previously the responsibility of the Third Sea Lord. The man appointed was Sir Eric Geddes, who became responsible for armaments production while the Third Sea Lord remained in control of naval weapons design. All this meant an expansion of naval and administration staff. These changes came at a time when the need for mines and depth charges was critical. There was a vast improvement in the production of mines but the case for depth charges was less impressive. By 1918, however, production of both weapons had increased enormously.

One of the more important departments of the Admiralty, the Inspectorate of Naval Ordnance, was also one of the newest. From 1 April 1908, the Admiralty assumed responsibility for inspecting its own ordnance. During this early period of its life, the Inspectorate was mainly concerned with the manufacture of guns and munitions for the navy; underwater weapons did not trouble them until the advent of the First World War. The main work of inspecting steels and gun barrels was based around Sheffield. More importantly, the department was heavily involved with research and experiment in forms of naval warfare.

In 1914 the Naval Ordnance Inspectorate was held in high esteem since the gun, the proven naval weapon, was expected to dominate naval warfare. The main research department had three branches: proof and experimental work, chemical research and mechanical research. It was originally under the control of an army officer, the Director of Artillery at Woolwich, which had become the home of test facilities for ordnance prior to the naval establishment. Woolwich manufactured many ordnance components, but not all. Usually,

One of the huge M class submarine monitors, which demonstrated the continuing obsession of the Royal Navy with surface gunnery. These vessels were meant to use a large-calibre gun as their main armament. M–3 was converted in the 1920s to lay mines from her casing. George Malcolmson Collection

private companies were also involved in the production of weapons and, if they were for the navy, officers from the navy inspected them before acceptance.

In 1909 the Director of Naval Ordnance had total responsibility for the design of ordnance and ammunition accepted for naval service. Torpedoes and sea mines were taken over by the Admiralty in 1910. This had an important bearing on the ability of the navy to accept ideas into the service without the interference of the Ministry of Munitions during the First World War. The fact that the navy was able to act as a separate entity – unlike the army – helped the Admiralty enormously because they were then able to develop weapons for their own purposes. Torpedoes and mines were completely independent and new designs could be introduced relatively quickly with the minimum of interference. At high level the Ordnance Board had representatives from all the services. The one anomaly in this was that the Chief Inspector at Woolwich was, at the start of the war, responsible for examining propellants, explosives and fillings. The Research Department were responsible for explosive components and the Royal Laboratory at Woolwich prepared systems.

During the First World War the role of Chief Inspector at Woolwich was taken over by the Director General of Munitions Inspection at Whitehall. This change heralded a period of chaos in the supply of munitions, exacerbated by interference from Lloyd George himself. However, naval experiments were helped by the creation of a drawing office in 1915, under the control of the Chief Inspector, and this gradually assumed the proportions of a design office. It is also significant that a Mines Inspection department was set up – in Victoria Street, London, under a Captain Engineer – but this was under the control of the Mining School at *Vernon*. All of this demonstrates the fragmentary nature of naval design and perhaps explains why the depth charge was relatively easy to design and implement. The left hand did not necessarily know what the right hand was doing and a small semi-independent department like the experimental mining school could develop its theories without any interference from bureaucrats in the government.

Sandown on the Isle of Wight was a pleasant place to holiday in the Edwardian period. For those who lived in London or the Home Counties, the Isle of Wight was a convenient haven of tranquillity; even now, certain parts of the island retain something of the feel of an unspoilt British holiday. It was at Sandown, while on holiday, that Taylor conceived the idea for the hydrostatic depth-charge pistol. To understand why he might have come up with this idea, we have to look at Britain in the period 1914–15. As we have seen, the submarine was just beginning to make itself felt. In the words of Sir John Ross:

> The sinking of the *Aboukir*, *Hogue* and *Cressy* by a German submarine in October, 1914, almost threw me into a panic. What was there to prevent a similar fate overtaking the battleships of the Grand Fleet?[3]

The concept of the island nation protected by the Royal Navy was then far stronger than it is today and members of the general public were all concerned to think how the submarine menace could be dealt with.

Walter Conan, an Irish inventor, had developed an explosive underwater projectile, which was tested by the Ordnance Board. He recalled a man whose description could well fit Taylor:

> In 1913, in the ordinary course of business, I came across a man who was of inventive nature, and at the same time a first class amateur mechanic; amateur in the sense that he did not work for monetary gain ... This man had been for a considerable time working in conjunction with a naval officer on the problem of operating explosives underwater at a prearranged depth, by a method other than electrical, and to a certain extent, he had undoubtedly solved the problem.[4]

Could this be Herbert Taylor? It is certainly possible that Conan met him because both were involved in designing underwater weapons and both had contacted the Admiralty to sell their ideas. Even if this was not Herbert Taylor, and it is just an uncanny coincidence, it demonstrates how many amateur engineers and designers were keen to develop weapons at this stage in the naval war. Conan's underwater exploding fuze was tested at Lydd; it is thought that the idea was considered, but not used.

The Home Fleet under way, the archetypal image of British naval power.   George Malcolmson Collection

At some point in May or June 1915, following his consideration of the submarine threat, Taylor conceived the idea of a hydrostatic pistol. He submitted his ideas to the Admiralty for consideration. They were acted upon, probably because of the desperate need for an improved form of explosive charge. He claims in a subsequent deposition that he had actually submitted a depth-charge design.[5] Admiral Sims, in his memoirs published as *The Victory at Sea*, said that he had once asked Admiral Jellicoe who was the real inventor of the depth charge. The answer was vague and unconvincing: 'No man in particular ... It came into existence almost spontaneously, in response to a pressing need.'[6]

According to Jellicoe, the requirement was recognized when the Grand Fleet was cruising in the North Sea:

> a submarine fired a torpedo at one of the cruisers. The cruiser saw the periscope and the wake of the torpedo, and had little difficulty in so manoeuvring as to avoid being struck. She then went full speed to the spot from which the submarine had fired its torpedo, in the hope of ramming it. But by the time she arrived the submarine had submerged so deeply that the cruiser passed over her without doing any harm. Yet the officers and crew could see the submerged hull; there the enemy lay in full view of her pursuers, yet perfectly safe! The officers reported this incident to me in the presence of Admiral Madden, second in command. 'Wouldn't it have been fine if they

had on board a mine so designed that when dropped overboard, it would have exploded when it reached the depth at which the submarine was lying?'[7]

According to Jellicoe, this chance statement had been the catalyst for the development of the depth charge. Generally it is attributed to George Callaghan, Jellicoe's predecessor, who voiced a requirement for the depth charge in July 1915.

As is often the case, a strange sort of synchronicity was going on, for Herbert Taylor had joined HMS *Vernon* in June 1915 and had already submitted a design for the depth-charge pistol. The Annual Report of the Torpedo School for 1916 details the types of depth charges being developed by the navy and it makes clear that the lanyard-operated types were developed shortly before the hydrostatically-operated ones. We know that Taylor worked on these, as well as the D-type. This weapon was hydrostatically operated, and that system became almost universally used. Since the pistol was basically the main functioning device in the weapon, I believe Taylor can be given credit, in conjunction with a naval officer called Alban L Gwynne, for designing the depth charge. Considering the work that Taylor did on later versions of the pistol, it appears that he should be given credit for inventing it. This does not take into account the countless other individuals who were involved in the testing and evaluation of the weapon, but Taylor invented the ball-and-sleeve device for the depth-charge pistol that was quite simply a great idea at the right time.

A word of explanation may be required here to clarify the terminology. Normally any explosive device consisted of a detonator, to create the initial explosion, and a primer – or explosive 'amplifier' – to make the main charge explode. A pistol was the name used for the mechanical device that struck the detonator and started the whole train of events. One would normally think of a fuze to do this job for an artillery shell or other projectile, but a pistol is a specific device and its name also represents the mechanical action. Hence in the case of the depth charge the weapon required two events to take place. The primer was kept apart from the pistol and they were moved together during the descent towards the required depth. The pistol fired on being actuated by a spring-loaded device at a pre-determined depth.

In 1918, it was said that the depth charge was probably the greatest offensive weapon developed during the First World War and the mine was the greatest defensive weapon. In both cases Herbert Taylor and Alban L Gwynne were involved. We will return a little later to Gwynne, who was the designer of the primer safety device used in depth charges. Since these contained a large amount of explosive when they came from the manufacturers and had to be handled several times before they arrived at their war stations, the possibility of explosion had to be minimized. It might be remembered that in 1950 it was exploding depth charges that caused the colossal explosion at Bedenham Pier, between Gosport and Fareham, when filled depth charges were being handled in ammunition lighters. The handling was blamed for setting off 13,000 tons of explosive.

Alban L Gwynne's invention prevented such a catastrophe. His device was designed to keep the primer and detonator a safe distance apart, not only while the underwater explosive device was on the ship but also for a pre-arranged time after the depth charge was released into the sea. Hydrostatic pressure eventually pushed the detonator into a cavity in the primer, which allowed the pistol to function (see illustration on p. 30).

HMS *Vernon* was the technical branch of the Royal Navy that dealt with torpedoes and mines. It started its life in 1872, shortly after the invention of the torpedo by Robert Whitehead, on the first of a series of hulks at Portsmouth. Originally known as the Torpedo School, it was to become a key centre for the study of electricity and its application in the navy. HMS *Vernon* became an independent command in 1876 and for many years was based upon the warship *Vernon* and the steam frigate *Ariadne* in an area known as Fountain Lake, which has since disappeared into the bowels of Portsmouth Dockyard.

Portsmouth plays a key part in the history of the weapons described in this book. It is on the south coast of England, the sea approach protected by the Isle of Wight just offshore. The entrance to Portsmouth Harbour is relatively narrow, but this opens into a fine sheltered harbour, flanked on one side by Portsmouth itself and on the other by the Gosport peninsula. Whale Island, in the northern part of the harbour, was the home of HMS *Excellent*, a gunnery school since the 1830s. When HMS *Vernon* left its hulks and was sited on land, it ended up on the Gunwharf, just next to the dockyard and now a modern shopping and residential area. On the opposite side of the harbour was the Royal Naval Armaments Depot of Priddy's Hard, run by the Admiralty from 1891. This depot was a key element in the testing and production of naval weapons and munitions.

In June 1915, Herbert Taylor joined HMS *Vernon* and within a few weeks three experimental pistol models had been made, to test his ideas. The trials of the charge were accepted and the design eventually became known as the D-type Depth Charge with Mark IV pistol. Upon completion of this work Taylor was retained, at the experimental commander's request, for further work in connection with mining and he was responsible for the conversion of the earlier A- and B-type depth charges to hydrostatic operation.

Late in 1915 other civilians were appointed to HMS *Vernon* and Taylor was then detailed to equip a mining workshop for experimental purposes. At this stage he took over as Workshop Manager, duties which he performed until 1921. What Taylor often called 'the department' was set up at first on HMS *Warrior*, HMS *Donegal* and HMS *Marlborough* (collectively known as *Vernon*), and twelve engineering assistants were allocated to the job. The *Warrior* was not satisfactory as the unit's base, since it was cramped and little machinery could be brought in. In 1917 the unit was transferred to Gunwharf and 'the department' was given a joiners' shop, which could be converted to a machine shop, and the first floor of No. 21 building as offices. This was obviously the position the mining school was in when the photograph of Taylor and the other staff was taken (see p. 20).

Taylor appears to have laid out the experimental unit, decided on the machines required and organized all the relevant facilities to get it running. The naval ordnance staff were moved out of the area and more provision was made for experimental work. This required tradesmen for milling, welding, machining and other tasks, and soon there were about a hundred people working in the department. It dealt not only with mines, but also with the maintenance and fitting-up of depth charges. With this additional responsibility, staff numbers grew until thirty more WRNS were drafted in to help with the workload.

Taylor later stated his role in the department during the war very simply: 'During hostilities all mining experimental work (with the exception of mine shell pressing) was carried out in the workshop under my supervision.' Taylor made this statement in a deposition in May 1939, in support of a claim for payment from the Admiralty for all his inventive ideas over his career.[8] It may be therefore that there was a certain amount of 'over-egging' to ensure that he was paid his due. His statement ignores all the hard work and assistance that the rest of the team no doubt brought to the department, and Taylor's depth charge idea still required the assistance of Gwynne to make it workable. Whatever the extent of Taylor's input, it is clear that he was highly thought of. Evidence of this can be seen in the Admiralty request for him to continue working for them into the Second World War despite his advanced years.

The torpedo lecture room at HMS Vernon *during the First World War.*

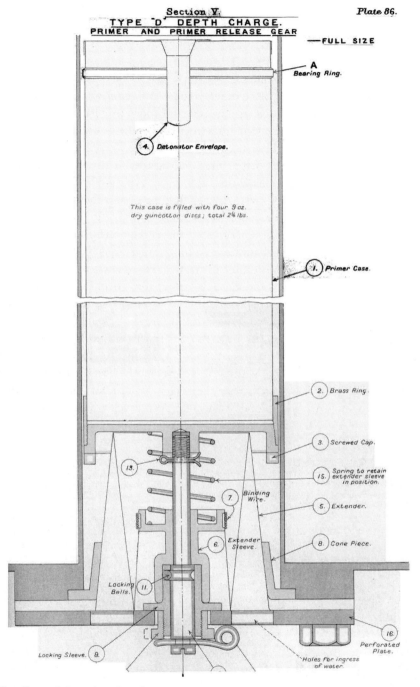

Alban Gwynne's invention, the safety primer gear.

The second member of the depth-charge team, and just as vital, was Alban L Gwynne. He was the naval officer who invented the safety primer device. Gwynne was born in 1880 and retired from active service at the age of forty-three with the rank of commander. He had been a midshipman on HMS *Caesar*, one of the old pre-dreadnought ships, in 1897. He had spent some of his career attached to the Turkish Navy around 1910 and eventually retired in 1915. This was timely, since in that year he was to work with Taylor on the perfection of the depth charge and his contribution, the safety primer. In 1924 he was recorded as living in Homewood, Esher, Surrey. It appears that Gwynne was also a prolific inventor and motoring enthusiast. He received a patent for anti-dazzle headlights for vehicles in 1924 (Patent number 247695). He had worked out that a series of shutters on a headlamp could deflect the bright glare of the lamps away from the vision of an oncoming motorist.

Gwynne stated that he had devised the primer safety device in May 1915, that a model was made of it about the end of May and that by the end of June the complete depth charges were being tested. His device, used in both the depth charge and the submarine mine, was hydrostatic and kept the primer, sometimes known as the booster, away from the detonator until it was required for use. This meant the explosive charge could safely be handled until it had been deployed from the vessel laying the mine. To quote from Gwynne's claim to the US authorities:

> Its importance in Modern Naval Warfare was however stressed by the British Naval authorities who had very recently adopted it as standard, and they placed before the US Naval Authorities two suitable forms of primer safety gear, viz.: that in the British Naval mines and that in the British Naval depth charge.[9]

Gwynne's device meant that the weapon would only operate at a set depth below the surface, and so safety and reliability were greatly improved. This might not be thought of great importance, but all the combatants in the First World War suffered from unreliable weapons, and more reliable weapons were more effective weapons. Gwynne claimed that the USA had copied his design and used it in their own mines. He claimed that the US Government should pay him $3 per mine for the first 5,000 made, $2 for the next 5,000 made and $1 each for any subsequent use. If 10,000 mines used his system, he would be entitled to $25,000, a colossal sum in those days. Commander Fullinwider of the United States Ordnance Bureau had also lodged a claim. Gwynne appealed against this in the United States. By an agreement of 14 July 1924, W S Ruckman of the US Patents Office, the Examiner of Interferences, awarded the patent rights to A L Gwynne.

The concept of the hydrostatic pistol was also used in naval howitzers. It was not such a strange idea that the gun could be utilized in the same way as

R. P. VISÉ PARIS 629

New weapon for use against submarines

A French submarine innovation, a quick-fire howitzer for use against submarines.

the depth-charge thrower and in many cases it was easier to convert an existing weapon than create a new one. The term 'howitzer' in this period normally described a short-barrelled gun that was normally elevated over 45° and fired at low velocity, so that the projectile trajectory was a high parabolic arc. The range was expected to be short, typically about 300 yards. If a weapon could be adapted to do this, then it could fire a heavy bomb. There were rifled and smooth-bore versions of the howitzer and both used a stick bomb with a hydrostatically operated pistol. There were three types of howitzer: 5-inch, 7-inch and 11-inch. The 11-inch howitzer was designed to throw a 600lb stick bomb loaded muzzle-first into the barrel of a conventional shell. An example of such a gun exists in the collection of the Museum of Naval Firepower in Gosport and the Admiralty manual belonging to the weapon states distinctly that it fired a 600lb bomb. As with the depth charge, the howitzer's projectile could be adjusted to explode at different depths. There were also 200lb stick bombs and 350lb bombs, depending on the weapon used. Unusual tactics were sometimes employed that were not normally envisaged for the naval howitzer. One such instance is cited in Jellicoe's book *The Crisis of the Naval War*. On 23 March 1918, a merchant ship managed to fire her 7$\frac{1}{2}$-inch howitzer at a torpedo approaching the ship from a range of 600 yards. The gunners fired a round that was seen to explode near the track of the torpedo:

A projectile fired from the howitzer exploded under the water close to the torpedo, deflected it from its course, and caused it to come to the surface some 60 yards from the ship; a second projectile caused it to stop, and apparently damaged the torpedo, which when picked up by an escorting vessel was found to be without its head.[10]

Chapter Three

Breakthrough! The invention of the depth charge

On 27 October 1914, the battleship *Audacious* struck a mine while on exercises off the coast of Ireland. The mine had been laid by an armed merchant cruiser called the *Berlin*. Losing a brand new battleship was a serious blow, but losing it to an underwater, unmanned explosive device – a tiny thing compared to the size of the ship – was alarming. It showed how deadly mines could be as a weapon, offensive as well as defensive. Once the *Audacious* had been sunk, it was clear to the government that the coastal waters of Britain would have to be swept regularly. A new kind of war had arrived – the underwater war.

In 1914, the mine was almost always moored, anchored to the sea-bed by a long cable. If this could be cut, the mine would float to the surface, where it could be detonated harmlessly, often by rifle fire; but first the mine had to be found. In the First World War, minesweeping typically relied on two ships towing between them a wide loop of cable attached to the stern of each ship. Normally the momentum of the sweep wire passing through the water was enough to cut a mine cable, but it was not unusual for a slow vessel to drag the mine and sinker along the sea-bed. In such a case, it would have to pull the mine to shallow water to expose and destroy it.

Minesweepers could also use the equipment fitted on trawlers to keep fishermen's nets at the correct depth, so the minesweeping cable was kept at the same depth. These devices were known as otters and resembled a sort of underwater kite. The otter was towed on a separate cable. In 1916, serrated minesweeping cables came into service. When these were towed through the water, they cut through any mine cables because normally the sweep wire was serrated to create a sort of sawing motion on the mooring cable. In principle, this was a simple method of sweeping, but it was quite complex to carry out efficiently. It relied on two vessels a certain distance apart, both steaming at a certain speed to maintain depth, with a certain amount of cable being paid out from the stern of each minesweeper.

Such crews risked their lives, as in this episode off Flamborough Head, Yorkshire:

HMS Audacious *sinking in the Irish Sea, with destroyers in attendance.* George Malcolmson Collection

I remember one evening when I was in the *Vindelicia*. We had swept up what was thought to be a new type of mine, and it was decided to try and make it safe while it was still floating in the water. The whole section of sweepers was under the cliffs at Flamborough, lying round the mine at a safe distance. The flagship's boat was lowered and two men, one stripped rowed to the mine. It was very cold at the time. The naked man went overboard, and everybody looked on breathless while wires were cut and the detonator was withdrawn with the aid of a marlin spike [!] and other tools after a long struggle. When it was done the boat returned to the trawler, and the trawler picked up the mine and brought it to Grimsby.[1]

It has been estimated that 5,000 ships carrying troops, food and munitions were required weekly to keep the British Isles supplied in the First World War, and an immense area of sea had to be swept. To keep shipping routes free of mines, exploratory sweeping was used. Each day, all sorts of ships sailed from anti-submarine bases to a specific area of water, where they would begin sweeping to all directions of the compass. If mines were found, the area would be closed to merchant shipping. Not only was this a problem for merchant ships, but large naval forces were tied up in this activity. The sinking of several ships in an area often indicated a minefield and in that case trawlers and minesweepers were ordered to the area to carry out a systematic sweep. Harbours were considered to be more important and their entrances were swept once or twice a day. Moored mines were vulnerable at low tide because they would show at or near the surface, so minesweeping at low tide was a tactic often used by minesweeper crews.

If mines could divert so much of Britain's war effort, destroying men and ships, and hurting morale, it was natural for the Admiralty to start doing the same to the enemy. In 1914, there were no vessels specifically designed to lay mines. Merchantmen and naval vessels had to be converted for the task. The impressed vessels ranged from the *Princess Margaret*, which could carry 420 mines, down to trawlers, widely used for this and each able to carry twenty-two to thirty mines. Luckily Britain had a large fleet of trawlers and they could be converted for minelaying fairly easily. In this period mines were laid from the ship's stern, normally using a system of rails about the same width as the sinker that the mine sat upon. The sinker had four small wheels on its base and, as the ship moved along, the mines would be pushed off these rails into the sea. The timing and the interval at which they were discharged were critical, so that the extent of the minefield and the distance between the mines would be known exactly.

The naval vessels used for the job were mainly cruisers and destroyers. In fact, twelve light cruisers and over twenty-five destroyers of the V and W classes were converted so they could lay mines. Among the warships fitted out for minelaying were HMS *London*, a battleship dating from 1899, HMS *Amphitrite* and *Euryalus*, two cruisers built in 1898 and 1891 respectively, and HMS *Apollo, Andromache, Intrepid, Iphigenia, Latona, Naiad* and *Thetis*, all from the Apollo class built in 1891.

The following minelayers were also used: the *Abdiel, Gabriel, Vanoc, Vanquisher, Venturous, Tarpon* (later to be used for trials with Herbert Taylor on board), *Telemachus* and *Meteor*. According to *Jane's Fighting Ships*,[2] quite a few

Testing a mine. This was one of the early 500lb mines in use in 1914. George Malcolmson Collection

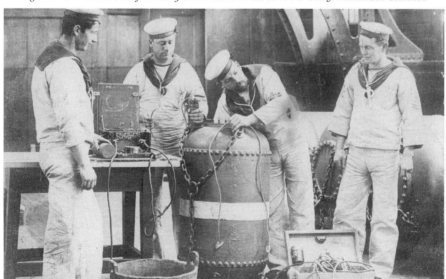

HM motor minesweeper No. 1. George Malcolmson Collection

other vessels were also fitted out for minelaying during the war. Coastal motor boats and auxiliary vessels carried mines for special purposes and there were the E and L class submarines which could carry mines in open tubes. The 1914–18 war also saw the first use of submarines to lay mines, which was a very risky business. Quite a few submarines were lost to this activity.

Despite such losses, the threat from mines did not lessen and 90 per cent of German mines laid in British waters were laid by U-boats, so there was no way of knowing where they were. Much naval warfare was now underwater, and it became more and more an anti-submarine war. The use of submarines as minelayers meant that the navy needed more minesweepers, and some anti-submarine tasks were allocated to these vessels as the war went on.

The German Navy was the first navy to authorize the widespread use of submarines in an offensive role in a major war. What kind of vessel did they employ? The standard U-boat could dive to 150ft and normally had two bow and two stern torpedo tubes. There were many marks and versions, but one of the commonest was the UB class, of which there were three marks. They had two 20-inch torpedo tubes and normally a 5cm gun. Thirty boats were built in the UBII class; only seven survived the war. It is said the UB submarines were built very quickly and were limited in their technical abilities. Nevertheless they could dive to a depth of 150ft, taking them out of range of the early forms of depth charge.

The UC minelaying submarines have already been mentioned. They had crew of 26 men and again could dive to about 150ft. Their armament was three 20-inch torpedo tubes and one 8.8cm gun, in addition to their mine complement. A major development in German submarines was the U-151 class cargo submarine or cruiser. Designed in response to the naval blockade of

German trade in 1915, they were introduced in 1917. With a length of 213ft, they were a radical departure from the coastal class of submarines. They were armed with two 20-inch bow torpedo tubes and two 15cm (or, in some cases, 10.5cm) guns and had a large hold for carrying stores and supplies. The diving depth was 195ft. Only seven were built.

A U-boat is not normally an armoured sea-going vessel. It is designed to use stealth and guile, relying on its guns and torpedoes to destroy enemy ships. Consequently the thickness of the hull is not very great. Even a small explosion near a submarine when under water may be enough to loosen its rivets and so cause leaks and damage to its structure, forcing it to the surface, where its opponents can deal with it more easily, or forcing it to dive deeper, causing more structural problems.

Normally a submarine was powered by a diesel engine on the surface and batteries driving electric motors when submerged. U-boats could run submerged for only a limited time. The batteries were fragile and full of acid. Destroy these and you disabled the vessel because it then had no underwater power. Hence came the idea of detonating an explosive charge on or next to a submarine, affecting the boat's structure and of course its crew's morale. A joint memorandum by the Planning Divisions of the British and American navies stated:

> The enemy must be brought to have a wholesome fear of coming within reach of our ships. It has been proved that depth charges exploded even within a radius of 1,000yd have an effect on enemy submarine morale, the effect of which cannot be over-estimated.[3]

To attack the submarine, specialized vessels were needed. The destroyer might seem the obvious choice, but in the First World War the destroyer was a general-purpose warship, not the improved anti-submarine vessel of the Second World War. Many destroyers were indeed used to patrol for U-boats, but they were used alongside a bewildering variety of other craft. Sloops were widely used, particularly the Flower class, which were much better than trawlers in an anti-submarine role. They were armed with two 4-inch guns, as well as a Hotchkiss 3-pounder and a depth-charge thrower. They had a single screw and could steam at 15 knots.

The P-boat was introduced during the war. It was designed to confuse a submarine, obviously not in the same way as a Q-ship, but by its low silhouette. Typically they were of about 600 tons displacement and 244ft long, with beam of 24ft and draught of 7ft 6in and at a distance they were hard to distinguish from submarines. They were fast, at 20 knots, and handled well even in rough seas. The P-boats had two 12-pounder of 12cwt guns and a single 4-inch gun, as well as two torpedo tubes and depth-charge throwers and racks. Smaller vessels were also employed: coastal motor boats and motor launches. These were very fast compared to the previous vessels, but could only be used in fair

P-32 and P-19. The P-class patrol boats were built to look like submarines and heavily armed for anti-submarine work. George Malcolmson Collection

seas. They could carry a 3-inch gun and several depth charges; the number varied over the course of the war. Most used depth charges of the D*-type designed for small-boat work. Taylor produced an improved version of the pistol in 1917, which allowed the depth charge to be fired at much greater depth. This eventually led to the abolition of the D* version, since even the smallest vessels could use the standard D-type.

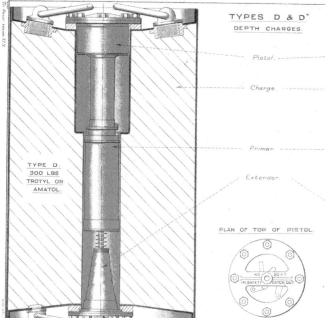

The D-type depth charge, showing the top of the pistol on the right.

Rear view of a P-boat towing a submarine. Note the depth-charge racks and Burney sweeps on their laying gear.

The use of submarines for minelaying just added impetus to the search for a viable anti-submarine weapon. When the threat of the submarine first became obvious, the Admiralty was bombarded with devices to combat it. One of many original madcap ideas, quickly discarded, was that of training seagulls to detect a submarine periscope and defecate on it, thus rendering the submarine blind! A bewildering variety of mines, nets and sweeps was put forward to the naval authorities and the problem was that most of them were ineffective.

One of the more sensible was the EC or electro-contact mine net, suggested by Admiral Sir A K Wilson VC. The combination of nets and mines was far more sensible than an unarmed net. While a net was a difficult obstacle to pass, it could be swept away by movement of the seas and required constant repair. Wilson's idea was to fix the mines to the net so that, as a submarine became enmeshed, the net would wrap around it, thus bringing the mines into contact with the hull. The British were going to use the mines as observation weapons, connected by a cable to the shore, where an observer with lead-acid batteries could explode the mine by remote control. After a great deal of experiment, it was decided to use empty mines to carry the batteries. These net devices were something of a failure: they do not seem to have hindered U-boats, though there were often claims that they did. HMS *Vernon* sifted through many schemes until they had identified those they thought would be practicable and of real benefit. Before the invention of the D-type depth charge, the Royal

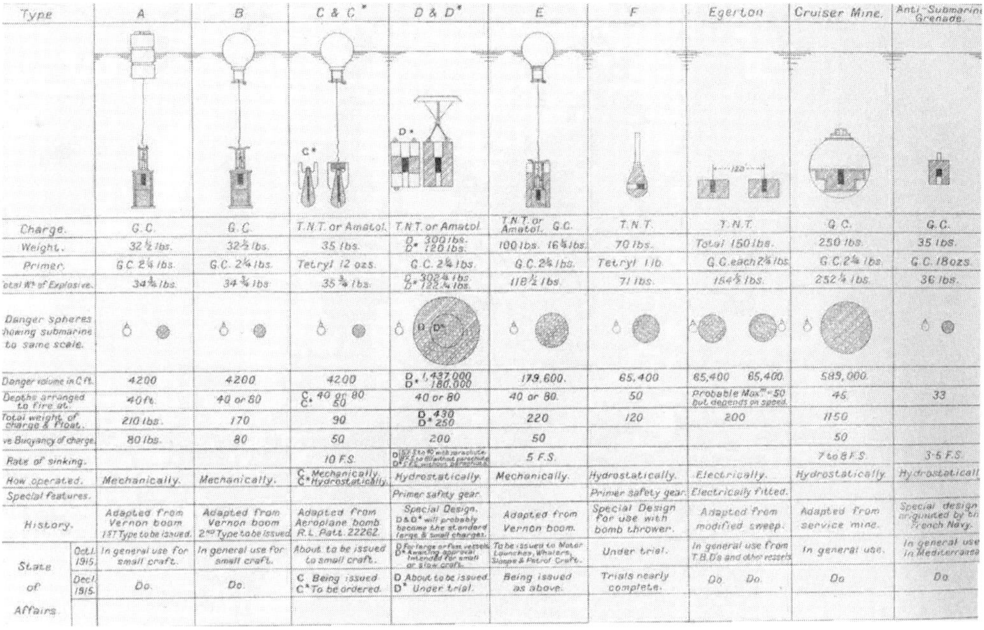

Type		A	B	C & C*	D & D*	E	F	Egerton	Cruiser Mine.	Anti-Submarine Grenade.
Charge.		G.C.	G.C.	T.N.T. or Amatol.	T.N.T. or Amatol.	T.N.T. or Amatol. G.C.	T.N.T.	T.N.T.	G.C.	G.C.
Weight.		32½ lbs.	32½ lbs.	35 lbs.	D. 300 lbs. D* 120 lbs.	100 lbs. 16¼ lbs.	70 lbs.	Total 150 lbs.	250 lbs.	35 lbs.
Primer.		G.C. 2¼ lbs.	G.C. 2¼ lbs.	Tetryl 12 ozs.	G.C. 2¼ lbs.	G.C. 2¼ lbs.	Tetryl 1 lb.	G.C. each 2¼ lbs.	G.C. 2¼ lbs.	G.C. 18 ozs.
Total Wt. of Explosive.		34¾ lbs.	34¾ lbs.	35¾ lbs.	D. 302¾ lbs. D* 122¾ lbs.	118½ lbs.	71 lbs.	154½ lbs.	252¼ lbs.	36 lbs.
Danger spheres showing submarine to same scale.					D D*					
Danger volume in C. ft.		4200	4200	4200	D. 1,437,000 D* 180,000	179,600.	65,400	65,400 65,400	589,000.	
Depths arranged to fire at.		40 ft.	40 or 80	C. 40 or 80 C* 50	40 or 80	40 or 80.	50	Probable Max.m 50 but depends on speed.	45	33
Total weight of charge & float.		210 lbs.	170	90	D. 430 D* 250	220	120	200	1150	
ve Buoyancy of charge.		80 lbs.	80	50	200	50			50	
Rate of sinking.				10 F.S.	D [illegible] with parachute [illegible] without parachute D* [illegible] without parachute	5 F.S.			7 to 8 F.S.	3·5 F.S.
How operated.		Mechanically.	Mechanically.	C. Mechanically. C* Hydrostatically.	Hydrostatically.	Mechanically.	Hydrostatically.	Electrically.	Hydrostatically.	Hydrostaticall[y]
Special features.					Primer safety gear.		Primer safety gear.	Electrically fitted.		
History.		Adapted from Vernon boom 1st Type to be issued.	Adapted from Vernon boom 2nd Type to be issued.	Adapted from Aeroplane bomb R.L. Patt. 22262.	Special Design. D & D* will probably become the standard large & small charges.	Adapted from Vernon boom.	Special Design for use with bomb thrower.	Adapted from modified sweep.	Adapted from service mine.	Special design originated by th[e] French Navy.
State of Affairs	Oct. 1915.	In general use for small craft.	In general use for small craft.	About to be issued to small craft.	D For large or fast vessels. D* Awaiting approval. Intended for small or slow craft.	To be issued to Motor Launches, Whalers, Sloops & Patrol Craft.	Under trial.	In general use from T.B.D's and other vessels.	In general use.	In general use in Mediterranea[n]
	Dec. 1915.	Do.	Do.	C. Being issued C* To be ordered.	D About to be issued. D* Under trial.	Being issued as above.	Trials nearly complete.	Do. Do.	Do.	Do.

This useful table describes all the early British depth charges. It is taken from the Annual Report of the Torpedo School, 1915.

Navy relied on sweeps and lanyard-operated charges. All these anti-submarine devices were developed by HMS *Vernon*.

The first type of depth charge seen in service in the Royal Navy, the A-type, was built in two parts. It consisted of a 32.5lb guncotton charge and a large float. The charge was enclosed in a steel drum, with a firing mechanism – normally known as the pistol – set into it. How far below the surface the charge sat was controlled by the length of the lanyard or line attaching the charge to the float. The charge was thrown overboard and sank, whereas the float remained on the surface. When the weight of the depth charge had extended the lanyard to its full length, the charge was pulled out of the pistol, which detonated it. Generally the depth setting was 40ft. The device was simple, but the depth setting could not be adjusted easily and it was woefully inaccurate.

Two more versions followed, known as B and C. The B-type had a slightly modified float and could be set to explode at 40ft or 80ft. The damage radius of the charge was thought to be 30ft. The C-type was a step further towards a weapon that could be used at various depths: the explosive case was designed to sink rapidly and was actually a modified 65lb aircraft bomb with the lanyard attached to the tail. It carried 35lb of amatol, a much more powerful explosive, and had a 12oz tetryl primer. Early depth-charge pistols were relatively simple and had a safety device or pin that would be removed before use. The system used a striker

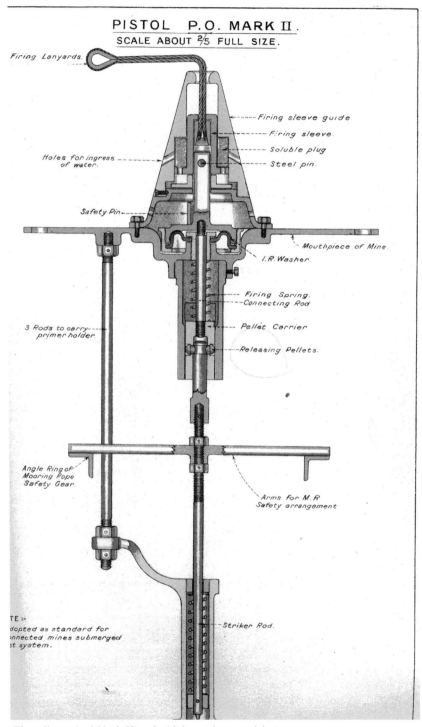

PISTOL P.O. MARK II.
SCALE ABOUT 2/5 FULL SIZE.

Firing Lanyards.

Firing sleeve guide

Firing sleeve.

Soluble plug

Steel pin.

Holes for ingress of water.

Safety Pin.

Mouthpiece of Mine.

I.R. Washer.

Firing Spring.

Connecting Rod

3 Rods to carry primer holder.

Pellet Carrier

Releasing Pellets.

Angle Ring of Mooring Rope Safety Gear.

Arms for M.R Safety arrangement

TE :-
dopted as standard for
nnected mines submerged
t system.

Striker Rod.

The pull-out pistol Mark II used with lanyard-operated devices.

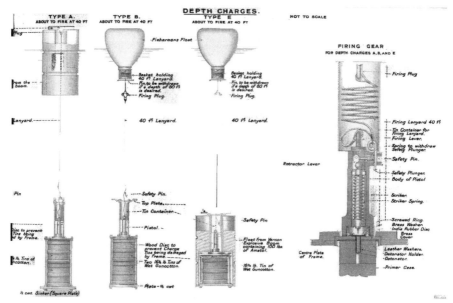

A-, B- and E-type depth charges and the firing pistol.

pin to hit the detonator and a spring to give the striker impetus. When the lanyard reached the end of its length, it compressed and then released the striker pin.

The later version of the C-type depth charge – known as the C* – was fitted with a hydrostatic pistol and this was a modification of Taylor's design. According to reports by HMS *Vernon*, it was to be issued after the D-type, suggesting it was a modification intended to use up existing stocks.[4] A post-war document from the Royal Commission on Awards to Inventors certainly supports Taylor's claim that he developed the conversion of C-type depth charges, and the conversion of B- and E-type depth charges subsequently known as the E* charge.[5] There were several problems with these weapons, mainly because they were vulnerable to mechanical damage: detonators or primers could easily be damaged in transit and the lanyard itself could snap on deployment, rendering the charge useless. They also had the drawback that they could be set only at defined depths, normally 40ft or 80ft.

The D-type was designed to replace the Egerton depth charge, designed by a naval officer of that name. It consisted of two electrically fired TNT charges, which would explode at 50ft. It was an idea adapted from the modified sweep, a device which was found serviceable but unreliable. The close similarity of design between mines and depth charges meant that the mine was inevitably seen as a cheap and widely available depth charge. Thus the cruiser mine was born: this was a mine adapted so that it could be dropped off the stern of a vessel and would explode hydrostatically at 45ft. Unfortunately, its round, traditionally mine-like shape made it very difficult to deploy and ships were fitted with special rigs to cope with it.

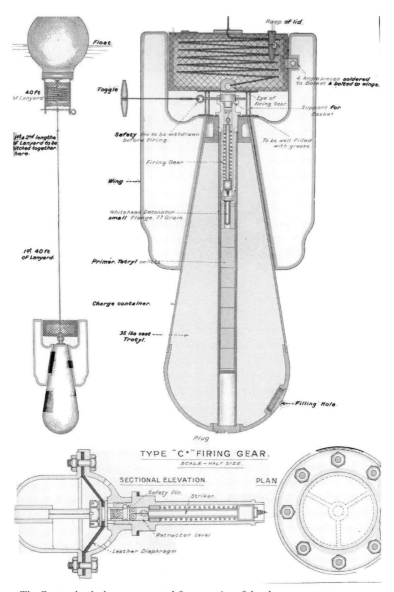

Hasp of lid.

Float.

40 ft of Lanyard

Toggle

4 Angle pieces soldered to Basket & bolted to wings.

Eye of Firing Gear

Support for Basket

Safety Pin to be withdrawn before firing.

1st & 2nd lengths of Lanyard to be hitched together here.

Firing Gear

To be well filled with grease.

Wing

Whitehead Detonator small flange 77 Grain.

1st 40 ft of Lanyard.

Primer Tetryl pellets.

Charge container.

35 lbs cast Trotyl.

Filling Hole.

Plug

TYPE "C" FIRING GEAR.

SCALE - HALF SIZE.

SECTIONAL ELEVATION.   PLAN

Safety Pin.   Striker.

Retractor Lever.

Leather Diaphragm

The C-type depth charge, converted from an aircraft bomb.

As early as 1913 some destroyers were being tested with laying gear that would separate the mine and sinker before launch, but it is not clear from the description in the Torpedo School report whether these conversions were intended for cruiser mines. The laying gear conversion was accepted and installed in all River class destroyers.[6] There were two marks of cruiser mine. The Mark I was a failure because, according to HMS *Vernon*, 'It was never a complete or entirely satisfactory design, but was hurriedly prepared and issued in the early part of the war.'[7] The Mark II was the one widely used by the Royal Navy. It had a Mark IV

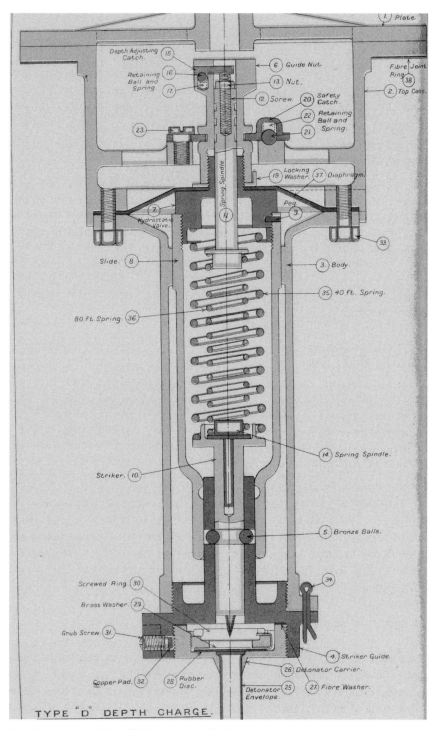

Depth-charge pistol Mark IV, showing the ball–release gear at point five.

HIGH SPEED SWEEP.

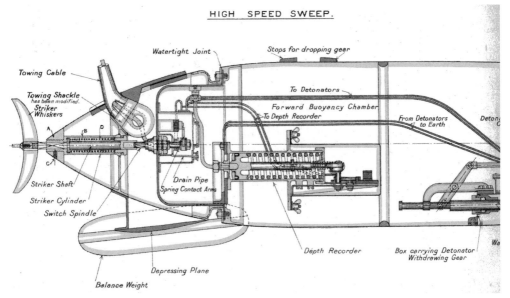

The nose of the high-speed sweep, with towing arm and firing mechanism.

mine pistol, a charge of 245lb wet guncotton and increased negative buoyancy, achieved by adding 120lb of lead in the bottom of the case.

One cannot discuss the invention of the depth charge without looking at the story of the explosive paravane. This anti-submarine weapon was the work of another prolific inventor, Lieutenant (later Commander) C Dennis Burney. As part of the work of the Anti-Submarine Committee, as a sub-lieutenant he was appointed in 1910 to HMS *Crusader*. The work carried out there eventually became embodied in the modified sweep, mentioned in Chapter One. He had an over-riding interest in aircraft and was visionary in prophesying, in a 1913 article in the *Naval Review*, that aircraft should be used to attack submarines. He left *Crusader* in 1911 and went on half-pay to carry out experimental work at Bristol, in concert with George White, whose purpose was to perfect a 'hydro-aeroplane'. In 1912 he attended HMS *Excellent* and trained as a naval gunnery officer. Patronage was still important in getting your ideas considered by the Admiralty and it was fortunate that Burney was able to call on the support of the Commander-in-Chief, Portsmouth.

Burney intended to try to solve the submarine attack problem by developing an explosive body towed at a constant depth underwater, 'unaffected by any variation of speed or helm'.[8] Burney was attached to HMS *Vernon* by dint of his connections with the Commander-in-Chief, Portsmouth, but he remained in command of HMS *Velox* so that he could conduct experiments from the ship. Initially, experimental models of his explosive weapon were made of wood and the hydrofoil sections were ordered from the manufacturing company of

HIGH SPEED SWEEP.

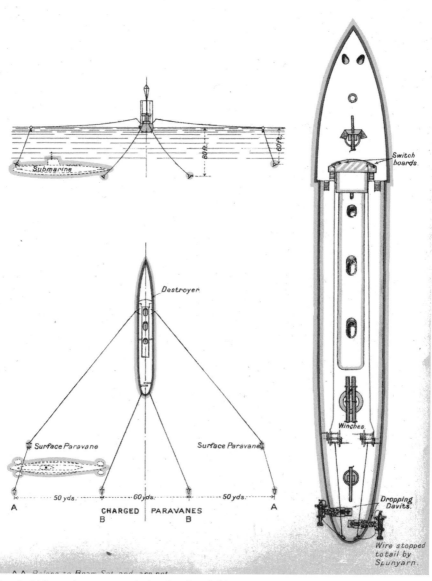

Plate 1ᴬ

Plate 1.

DIAGRAM OF SWEEP.

GENERAL ARRANGEMENT OF STERN SWEEP.

How the high-speed sweeps were deployed on board ship.

HIGH SPEED SWEEP.

FIRING BOARD.

PLAN AND SECTION THROUGH STAYS.

The Burney high-speed sweep and operating board, for firing on board ship.

George White in Bristol. Trials were carried out on the *Velox*, at first with a paravane and a surface hydroplane unit, but the latter was soon dispensed with when it was found to be superfluous. The end result of Burney's efforts was something that looked like a torpedo with wings. It became known as the paravane, or high-speed sweep.

Burney had submitted several ideas for towed paravanes in 1914, but his design could be used against mines as well as submarines. After the loss of HMS *Audacious*, this seemed a far more important idea than had previously been thought. The paravane – a torpedo-shaped weapon with a hydroplane attached to the front – was towed behind the ship and its 400lb explosive charge could be detonated by contact with the enemy vessel or by remote control by an operator in the stern of the ship. Burney adapted many of the ideas on the motion of bodies through water that he had developed during his seaplane trials.

Following the trials in February 1915, a set of Burney sweeps was fitted to HMS *Mastiff* and in due course an order was placed for forty-eight boats to be fitted with the system. The sweep could be fitted on the stern or on either beam. This would theoretically allow four sweeps to be fitted to each vessel, but generally there were only two. The sweep would maintain a certain depth when being towed and would veer away from the side of the ship. It could be deployed quickly when required. Generally, if it snagged a submarine, the paravane was drawn along its own cable until it came into contact with the submarine, at which point it was exploded. There were several types of paravane and various sizes of towing wire, depending on what was required.

Once the paravane had been accepted for service use, HMS *Vernon* contacted private industry to get the components manufactured. In reality, Burney was tasked with organizing his own scheme with the (limited) resources of HMS *Vernon* available to him. This was the catalyst for what became the Paravane Department, the grandiose name for a small group of individuals. At this stage they worked in a tiny first lieutenant's room in *Vernon* known as 'the oven'. In the early days, nine men were involved in the paravane department – a commander, two lieutenants (Burney and Bowles), one warrant officer, two petty officers, two sailors and one shorthand writer. Burney may have moved heaven and earth to get his idea into service, but the people who had to use it were less than impressed:

> We hated the contrivance, which was difficult to use, and always going wrong. Moreover the ship had to ease down when the sweep was being got in or out, which was always a risk if a submarine was in the vicinity. Added to this no commanding officer felt happy with two explosive objects towing behind his stern. There was the chance that they would be forgotten in a sudden emergency.[9]

However, the real requirement of the navy was an explosive charge that could be dropped and would explode correctly without intervention from the

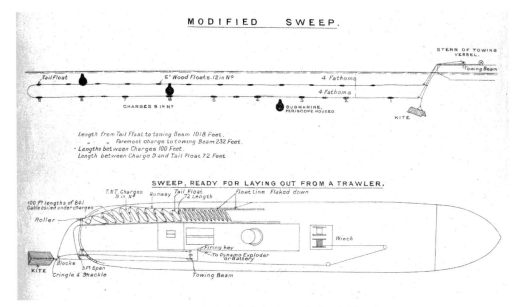

The modified sweep as laid out on a ship's deck (below) and deployed (above).

ship: the need for simplicity was of paramount importance. There are no definite accounts of the successful use of the paravane to sink a submarine, although at least fifty-three units were detonated. The nearest thing to a decisive kill was the action in which HMS *Ariel* is thought to have used an explosive paravane and depth charges to destroy the submarine UC-19. The early depth charges as they were called were notoriously unreliable. All the early submarine weapons – the explosive sweep, the modified sweep and the lanyard-operated depth charges – were of dubious value and as we have seen they were difficult to deploy.

It would also be disingenuous to heap all the praise for the development of a reliable weapon on one man, but it is equally difficult to give the credit to anyone else. For example Percy Scott, the great gunnery reformer, had some ideas on attacking submarines with explosives – as many people did in this period – but he did not design or produce an effective anti-submarine weapon that could be used with consistent effect.[10] Herbert Taylor was probably the most heavily involved in developing the firing mechanism and improving the weapon, but he was only one of many people who tested the weapon and manufactured the components. Alban L Gwynne was also an important contributor: his safety primer design ensured the depth charge could be used with minimal risk, since it was not armed until the point of use.

What explosives were available at this time? Most bombs and shells were filled with an explosive that was not liable to immediate detonation, one that required an initiator or intermediary explosive to set it off. Obviously this reduced the risk of premature explosion. Lyditte was one of the earliest such explosives – after gunpowder or 'black powder' – and was formed by the action of sulphuric or nitric acid on carbolic acid derived from coal tar benzene. It was so named because it was first tested on a site near the River Lydd. By the end of the nineteenth century, it was one of the main explosives in use. During the First World War trinitrotoluene or TNT, superseded it.

To make TNT, toluene is treated with sulphuric or nitric acid and forms a pale yellow crystalline solid, which is not affected by moisture. TNT has a melting point between 79° and 80°C. It is very stable and extremely powerful and was just coming into use in 1914. A derivation of TNT was amatol, which was a mechanical mixture of ammonium nitrate and trinitrotoluene in 60/40 proportions. Amatol was used for filling mines and projectiles in both world wars. The advantage of amatol was that it was less sensitive than TNT.

Because these explosives are stable in a normal environment, they require a chain of explosive events to happen before they are set off. In naval terminology these were known as the initiator and the intermediary. The initiator was a small quantity of a material such as lead azide or fulminate of mercury, which if struck mechanically would detonate. These types of chemicals were used inside the detonator but, being extremely sensitive, they were used in small quantities. The initiator set off a small explosion and the intermediary, typically composition exploding powder (picric powder), acted as an explosion amplifier and accelerated and intensified the detonation to such a level that they set off the main charge.

The depth charge itself was not complicated. It consisted of four parts: the explosive charge, the pistol, the casing and the safety primer. The latter was meant to keep the charge safe until the moment of use. Early attempts at developing explosive charges such as this were problematic, because the pistol could not stand the impact of hitting the water and could explode as soon as the charge was launched – an obvious risk to the crew! All fuzes and explosive initiators require some form of safety mechanism.

The trials of the depth charge between 1915 and 1916 were extensive and laborious. The manual still exists that detailed the types of trials carried out and many of the books bound within it are full of sketches of the weapon, the way it was laid, its attitude on firing and many other details. The pistols themselves were subjected to rigorous tests to see how they behaved when subjected to stresses beyond what they would receive in service. The idea for a pistol was submitted to the Admiralty in 1915, but it was Taylor, the practical engineer, who could produce working models of his ideas for the Admiralty in his workshop. He did so on 10 July 1915. Taylor was about to demonstrate that his mechanical genius could produce new and more powerful weapons; it says much for the Admiralty that they trusted him to produce the parts needed for trials.

Gwynne later stated that his part in the story began in May 1915, when the Admiralty asked him to produce a depth charge having a safety primer device.[11] It was with Captain H L Skipworth of the Torpedo School that his idea was developed. Gwynne was working at the Admiralty on the depth charge and hit upon a way of making it safe once dropped off a ship. He was in charge of the department responsible for submarine mining, under the overall command of Captain Skipworth. In his deposition for a patent in the United States, Gwynne stated:

> I remember distinctly examining the forces that were available to operate a primer safety gear. I remember, for instance, discarding the gravity arrangement and I remember deciding that the use of hydrostatic pressure was most practical and would probably prove practicable.[12]

Within a few weeks of 1 May 1915, apparently, Gwynne had produced a model of the safety device for analysis. The depth charge was first tested at Portsmouth at the end of June. On 13 December 1915 trials were carried out, from No. 1 steamboat, on the pistol and primer. The idea was to establish what would happen if the depth-charge primer were in the safe position and the detonator was then activated. The depth charge was filled with sand and the detonator contained fulminate of mercury, while the primer had $2\frac{1}{4}$lb of dry guncotton. Guncotton is the material that results when cellulose, under the action of strong nitric acid, produces a nitric ester called nitrocellulose. The cellulose in this case was cotton and guncotton was a very unstable kind of explosive, but it worked well in primers.

The charge was placed in water at a depth of about 40ft and the result was that 'a considerable quantity of bubbles appeared on the surface. This presumably was air from the case and gases from the detonator. No smoke appeared, and there was practically no noise'.[13] It was found that the guncotton was untouched when the safety primer was in the safe position. However, the welded seams of the charge case had opened and also part of the bottom of the case was torn away from the sides. The observers, Petty Officer Osborne and a Mr Pratt of the Mining School, dryly observed that the remarkable strength of the 778rs detonator should be noted. A similar trial was tried out at Horsea the same day to ascertain how the arrangement would react in air; water pressure was applied by a pump. In this case the primer exploded completely, destroying the charge case and everything in it and this flummoxed the officers in charge.

Next day the commander of HMS *Vernon*, together with Alban Gwynne, Commander Holbrook and Lieutenant Commander Sherman, carried out four runs on HMS *Wizard* to determine the firing capabilities of the D-type depth charge. Two runs were made at various speeds between 6 and 20 knots, and two more at a steady speed; at 20 and 10 knots, the depth was set at 40ft, whereas on the other runs it was set at 80ft. The two charges dropped at 40ft both had parachutes attached. In all cases, the charges went off 11–15 seconds after they had been dropped. The observers commented: 'The shock appeared to be more severe when the setting was set for 80′. This setting was therefore taken for the slowest speed.'[14] It was concluded that the depth charge was completely acceptable and that the minimum speed for laying was 6 knots.

In January 1916, Herbert Taylor, Lieutenant Commander Leatham and Petty Officer Osborne began trials to find out the safe distance from the primer at which the detonator could be fired, as a continuation of the December trials. The primer was fitted in a steel tube along with an electrically fired detonator. It was found that the addition of an asbestos disc to the primer considerably reduced the chances of a premature explosion. The optimal distance between primer and detonator was considered to be 3in. The general conclusion was that 'the margin between the safe and unsafe distance of the detonator away from the primer is very critical'. Further testing went on in February 1916 to establish the best kind of valves to use with the pistol and a firing trial was carried out on 17 February 1916.

Trials continued on the pistol Mark I, which had been modified because of early problems with the ball-release mechanism. Taylor and Osborne were out on the *Skylark*, a 302-ton motor launch, on 14–15 February to test the modified version. After fourteen separate tests, they found that the modification had worked as a far greater uniformity of firing was achieved. It is interesting to see how this was done, because the timing of the firing was crucial. According to the trials' report, the time-recording device was an instrument used for depth-sounding bombs but the officer, in this case Taylor, had to indicate visually when dropping the pistol. Therefore, when it was found that the pistols fired a little earlier than expected, the conclusion was that this might have been due to human error.

The use of the old lanyard-operated types of depth charge was not dismissed and accordingly, on 17 February 1916, Taylor – along with Commander Russell and Mr T Chandler from the Mining School – embarked on board the trawler *Shackleton* in order to test C-, C*-, D- and E-type charges. The ship cruised at between 6 and 8 knots and various depths were tried: the two C-type charges were dropped at depths of 40ft and 50ft and they fired after a time lapse of 4.4 seconds. In comparison, the D-type was dropped at a speed of 8 knots and exploded after 13.6 seconds. When the E-type was tried, it failed to fire. Since the pistol had just been received from the manufacturers and was the first of its type, the officers concluded that poor workmanship was responsible for the failure.

In October 1917, trials continued to find out how the charge would behave in the first 20ft of the descent. On two runs carried out on 5–6 October, charges were dropped vertically, with the pistol at the top, and then with the pistol arranged horizontally. From these trials, depth/time graphs were calculated and it was established that the charges stabilized in a horizontal position on their descent. The vertically dropped charges sank rapidly at first and then turned to the horizontal. Trials carried out in a similar way from HMS *Acteon* determined at what height the charge could be dropped from the ship without the pistol firing. It was found that charges could be dropped from 35ft without detrimental effect. Further trials in November 1917 concluded that they could be dropped from a height of 50ft with safety. Since water is incompressible, it acts as a hard surface. A solid object that hits the water from a height at a certain speed is likely to suffer damage. If this phenomenon can break human limbs, it can also damage a metal object and perhaps make it ineffective.

The trials of the depth charge had proved to be successful in many ways, but even as late as 22 November 1917 Lieutenant Commander Murray in Coastal Motor Boat No. 18 did not get the results that were hoped for. The boat carried four D-type charges with Mark II pistols. Two were carried with pistols facing forward and two with pistols facing aft. They were dropped at a speed of 35 knots in 15ft of water and none of them fired. It seemed therefore that the pistol was limited in its ability to fire in shallow water. For this reason a Mark V pistol was developed for shallow firing. It eventually needed a balance weight to overcome the shock of dropping, since it was more sensitive than the other versions.

A Mark VI pistol was developed, but this was meant for situations where a wider range of shallow-depth settings was needed. It had a large dome with four settings on the adjuster. After tests, a second version of this pistol – called the Mark VI* – was introduced that was thought to be free from inertia firing and was considered to be far easier to use on the forebridge of the ship. This pistol brought together the two designers who for a long time were designing independently but for the same organization. Both Sturgeon and Taylor were awarded a payment by the Royal Commission on Awards for Inventors in 1920. In clause B, the Mark VI is covered by the phrase 'conjointly with Mr R A Sturgeon late of the Mining School, and now of 7 Hillhurst Avenue, Chapeltown, Leeds'.[15] This has some relevance for it is known that Sturgeon too attempted to patent the depth-charge pistol Mark VI.

The same document summarized the numbers of different types of pistols produced for the war effort. Of the early versions, 1,000 of the Mark I were produced, 20,000 Mark IIs, only 100 Mark IIIs and 70,000 Mark IVs. Two types of primer safety gear were produced: one with the ball-release mechanism, of which 3,600 were made, and one an adaptation that Taylor had patented, which was the primer safety gear with a rolling rubber ring. Altogether 12,000 of these devices were made and this appears to demonstrate that Taylor was able to improve upon Gwynne's initial design; at the same time he was able to reduce the cost of manufacture by half. This ability to reduce the cost of manufacture seems to have been a feature of Taylor's career and one that would make him valuable to the Admiralty.

To get a depth charge into the sea, it needs some sort of delivery mechanism. This could be as simple as a set of rails along which the charge rolled off the stern of the vessel, but ideally it required a thrower or low-velocity gun to hurl the charge clear, so the vessel had enough time to pass out of danger. The Thornycroft Company first introduced depth-charge throwers, made at its works at Woolston near Southampton. These enabled naval vessels not only to drop their charges from the stern of the ship but also to fire them out to the sides. It is thought that the Commander-in-Chief of Portsmouth, Admiral Stanley Colville, was the first to come up with a proposal for the thrower. In a very short space of time, the thrower was ready for service, in July 1917.

The propulsion system had to create a large enough detonation to push the charge high into the air and clear of the ship. The charge itself was mounted on what was known as an arbor. In the earliest versions, this was a sort of half-tray wrapped around the body of the charge. It had a wooden plug fitted to the underside, which fitted into the barrel of the thrower. The arbor was sacrificial – once the thrower had fired, the arbor was lost. When the thrower fired, they separated in flight, the arbor imparting just enough thrust to send the charge on its way. The thrower was eventually to consist of a cast-iron tube with a breech and firing mechanism. The development of the throwers was almost exclusively given to the Thornycroft Company, whose head, John Thornycroft, was heavily involved in trials. What might seem little more than a simple smooth-bore gun was a more complex installation than one might imagine. For example, the thrower used an explosive cordite charge in a propellant case and the stress on the deck of the ship and the weight of the equipment had to be considered.

If a U-boat was being chased, the commander of the vessel had to guess its track, set a course along the suspected path and then drop charges along it. The throwers, when fired from the sides of the vessel, were especially useful if the U-boat changed course. If four throwers were fitted, they would be fitted to each quarter. Trials of the depth-charge thrower began when Thornycroft delivered a prototype, based on a similar weapon they had prepared for land service. The thrower's purpose was to widen the area dangerous to any underwater enemy craft. It fired a depth charge to a range of 40yd. The charge size was critical and an extra ounce of powder could extend the range out to 80yd.

Loading time for the thrower was about $1\frac{1}{2}$ minutes. Later in the war, when the hydrophone became developed, the rate of fire was much improved. The hydrophone was a towed array, so the charges needed to be dropped in one attack rather than as single charges widely spaced. Some throwers, fitted with a quick-loading sleeve for the breech and a ready-loaded rack, could achieve a rate of fire of six charges per minute. The hydrophone affected the way that depth charges could be used tactically, because the noise of the explosion hindered the hydrophone operator. These improvements were all designed in such a way that depth charges released from the throwers would explode at the same time as those from the rails.

In June 1918, Lieutenant Commander Tooth carried out extensive tests at Eastney proving ground to establish the size of the cordite charge needed to get the depth charge out to a range of 80yd. Representatives were sent from HMS *Excellent* and Woolwich Arsenal. This was an interesting experiment because it used Cordite MD. It had been found that early forms of cordite were corrosive and damaged the barrel of a gun, so MD (for 'modified') was developed to counter this. The test used crusher gauges in the cartridge containers and in the barrel and cartridge chamber.

Crusher gauges were small devices for measuring the force of an explosion. They were used for internal ballistic measurement. A crusher gauge consisted of a small steel vessel containing a copper tube, the vessel closed by a screw gland in which a piston with a defined surface area was placed. This piston was covered by a gas check that prevented explosive gases entering the cylinder. On firing, the pressure exerted on the gas check, and thus on the copper cylinder, was uniform and so the internal gas pressure could be measured by the extent that the copper tube had been crushed. The maximum range achieved was 103yd with 7oz of cordite MD 8. HMS *Brazen* also tested the effect of the added range in relation to the orientation of the charge. This was critical to the damage that could be sustained via the primer on impact, and the longer range also affected on the force on impact, since the carrier weighed 150lb.

Three technical innovations were being tried out before the war ended: the hydraulic firing of throwers from the forebridge; the testing of extended-range throwers; and the development by Thornycroft of a guide-loading breech. Hydraulic firing of the throwers became a critical piece of the system, because the timing of firing was very important in a successful depth-charge attack. The staff at *Vernon* tested Taylor's design and his equipment was then sent on to Thornycroft for manufacture. In every part of depth-charge design, even of the thrower, we see Taylor being allowed to comment on its suitability or else design something new.

Trials of the bomb gun were carried on at Horsea Island in January 1916 to see if the accuracy and time of loading were affected by various conditions. During these trials, the throwers used a pneumatic arrangement with carbon dioxide as the propellant. The maximum range was 152yd with a gas pressure of 530lb per square inch. All these trials revealed problems to be overcome. There were sealing problems between the charge and the thrower, which were affected by the leakage of grease and water. In fact, water was found inside the barrel of the thrower. Loading was speeded up by recharging from both carbon dioxide cylinders at once. Carbon dioxide was considered useful as being a non-explosive propellant, but its habit of frosting up when the bottles were depleted gave problems in service.

When the Admiralty finished the trials and accepted the weapon for service, they sent the following communication to Thornycroft, on 6 July 1917:

> Gentlemen, I am commanded by my Lords Commissioners of the
> Admiralty to state that they have before them the particulars of the
> bomb throwers manufactured by you and a report of the trials which
> were successfully carried out at Portsmouth. Their Lordships desire
> to convey to you an expression of their appreciation for the able

production of so valuable a weapon. I am Gentlemen, Your obedient servant

J B Abraham.[16]

The final chapter of the Experimental Mining School's life came when the Admiralty decided to amalgamate it with the Paravane Department. There was no mention of Herbert Taylor in the lists, but by this time he had moved to other duties and those whose position or salary was unchanged were not mentioned in the report. Taylor set up a motor engineering company with his son but he appears to have still been working for the Admiralty even though he had a business. This may have been to supplement his salary. There is an interesting document in the Public Record Office that deals with the amalgamation and gives us some idea of the organization as it stood at the end of the First World War.

According to this document, 'The Mining School has been to a great extent an organisation for War and it may be expected to reduce very considerably in Peace conditions. The basis on which it should be finally organised for Peace must be a matter for further close investigation on data which are not at present known'.[17] From this and other comments it can be seen that the people and posts mentioned in the document had been geared for high productivity in war. The Commander-in-Chief of HM Ships and Vessels in Portsmouth had, through the Captain at HMS *Vernon*, considered himself fortunate to be able to retain staff on a temporary basis and at a lower pay rate than they had had in wartime.

The question of pay was a thorny one. Draughtsmen working for the Mining School and the Paravane Department had disputed their weekly base rates. Through the offices of the Association of Engineering and Shipbuilding Draughtsmen, they were demanding more money and the situation had not been resolved by 25 October 1918.[18] The implication from the correspondence discussing these issues between the Captain of HMS *Vernon*, the Superintendent of Mining and the Commander-in-Chief was that they wanted men on six or twelve-month contracts and a rate less than that paid during wartime. Considering these men's contribution to the war effort, they do not seem to have been regarded very highly.

Apart from the draughtsmen, only two individuals were asking for pay rises and one was an academic, a Dr Walker, whose salary was going to rise from £500 to £800 a year. It is not that surprising then that people such as Gwynne and Taylor pursued private payments for inventions or that Taylor was somewhat aggrieved that his status never altered during his early career at the Mining School. Of the eighteen Royal Naval Volunteer Reserve staff at the School and in the Paravane Department, the majority were earning about £500 a year. The two civilian engineers quoted in the report were to have their salaries raised from £350 to £500 a year. The following RNVR Officers were employed at the Mining School at this time:

Lieutenant F P Pickford, Assistant Director, Section T.2
Lieutenant G F Turner, Technical Secretary
Lieutenant F J Tindall, Electrical Engineer Section T.2
Lieutenant A R Menderson, Engineer in charge of Design
Lieutenant E Gilmore, Mechanical Engineer Section T.2
Lieutenant L J Ashby, Visiting staff
Lieutenant P H Liniley, Mechanical Engineer Section T.2
Lieutenant A H Reeve, Mechanical Engineer Section T.2
Lieutenant A L Anthony, Assistant to Engineer in charge of Design
Lieutenant G S Garner, Assistant for Special Duties with depth charges
Lieutenant A D Alexander, Engineer in Depot Section
Lieutenant J C Prescott, Electrical Engineer, Section T.2
Lieutenant M Heary, Engineer, Paravane Department
Lieutenant C M Lander, Engineer, Paravane Department
Lieutenant G Cook, Engineer, Sweeping Section
Warrant Armourer F Andrews, Foreman of Trades
Assistant Artificer Ashcroft, Junior Engineer, workshop
Chief Petty Officer J W Horner, Junior Engineer, Electrical section

The men whose status was unchanged were not mentioned in this document, except for the two civilians, Mr C E Davies and Mr W R Steele. Davies was the former Engineer in charge of design. He replaced Mr R A Sturgeon, one of the key figures in this story and inventor of the buoyant sinker (which floated briefly before filling with water and sinking to the sea-bed) and of the mine design that became almost universal in the Second World War. Sturgeon had been promoted, but the only record of him here is that he was then on a salary of £500 a year. All these men worked for the Superintendent of Mine Design, who at that time was one of the senior staff.

It is an interesting if unpalatable fact that there were two processes by which the Royal Navy accepted new ideas at this period. When ideas came from the upper ranks, or those connected with them, the Admiralty was much more likely to implement an invention. An order would be given by one of the sea lords for a new item to be produced; if the navy could not produce it, they would go to an outside contractor through the Director of Contracts. If the idea came from the lower ranks, from an NCO or a civilian in a naval department, the procedure was more complex.

Any proposal could be sent to the Secretary of the Admiralty, normally by the commanding officer of the establishment. The idea would then be forwarded to the relevant departments. This normally meant that it would go to the departmental registry, and from there to the official concerned. Once the relevant departments had been consulted and had commented on the idea, the document was returned to the Third Sea Lord. If, after his consideration, he thought it was a good idea, it was sent back to the secretary who was told to 'make it so'. The difficulty for the unconnected was that at any point some individual could foul up the process. If you were protected by a senior naval figure, this was far less likely to happen.

Generally an instruction came all the way back to the originating institution, where they were expected to do several things: create a design, write a specification and get the drawings of the device drawn up. When all this was done, it went through the same procedure as the initial idea, back to the Sea Lord, where it had to be approved again. The Contracts Department would then issue the private contractors with the drawings and specifications and ask for a tender. They normally took the lowest price. All this took time and it was not unusual for the inventor to try to take short cuts to enable their project to be completed if agreed.

There is an interesting parallel here between Dennis Burney and Herbert Taylor. Burney was well connected: his father was Admiral Sir Cecil Burney, who just happened to have been the first President of the Anti-Submarine Committee. There is little doubt that Burney would be listened to when he came up with new ideas. This is only part of the story, because Burney was a driven man and obsessed with the idea of aircraft and weapons in the navy. He gave a great deal of time and effort to perfect his ideas and at the end of it all did not expect payment from the navy. He did, however, eventually gain from the ability to sell his ideas abroad and get a payment from the Admiralty.

Chapter Four

Depth charges, throwers and pistols

In studying the historical development of the depth charge as a ship-borne anti-submarine weapon, it is remarkable how little the basic design has altered since its inception in 1915.[1]

The Imperial War Museum is full of images of the Battle of the Atlantic during the Second World War, and films of fleet escorts rushing in to attack U-boats are common. Crews shrouded in overcoats, and buffeted by winds on huge green seas, wrestle with mechanical devices on the rear of their ship and deliver what appear to be oil drums over the stern of the ship. Those drums are the ubiquitous depth charge Mark VII, which was basically a 132kg charge of explosive set off by a pistol that went off at a given depth, actuated by a hydrostatic device set on deck before release. The Mark VII, the standard depth charge in the second war, was derived from the D-type and this chapter looks at the development from one to the other.

The depth charge is not a particularly new idea and it had been known for some time that the effect of an underwater explosive charge on a ship's side was enough to sink it or severely disable it. The Admiralty established an Anti-Submarine Warfare Committee in 1910 in response to the new threat.[2] The D-type was the first hydrostatically operated depth charge that was essentially designed by Taylor and Gwynne, and their design stood the test of time. The depth charge consisted of a metal drum filled with explosive and a detonating unit or pistol as it was known. The pistol was operated by water pressure and it is this device which Herbert Taylor designed.

The earliest models of D-type used a steel parachute to control the rate of sinking: they too could only operate at a depth of 40ft or 80ft. Although this might seem like little improvement on the earlier types, the fact that a hydrostatic switch operated it made the whole unit far more effective. The D*-type was a version for vessels that were considered to have insufficient speed to drop the heavier D-type depth charge safely. Its damage zone (then called the 'explosive radius', but measured in cubic feet) was very much smaller.

The answer to the submarine? A depth-charge explosion at a depth of probably 80ft, despite what the caption says. George Malcolmson Collection

The two D-type depth charges

Type	D	D*
Charge	TNT or amatol	TNT or amatol
Weight	300lb	120lb
Primer	guncotton 2¼lb	guncotton 2¼lb
Damage zone	1,437,000 cu. ft	180,000 cu. ft
Depth	40ft to 80ft	40ft to 80ft
Total weight	430lb	250lb
Rate of sinking	15ft per second	5ft per second
Operation	hydrostatic	hydrostatic

The pistol itself consisted of a detonator and carrier with two operating springs, one each for the different depth settings, as well as a striker, with gunmetal housing and hydrostatic valve. For operation, the safety catch had to be set to the 'out' setting. Once the depth charge was immersed in water, the pressure operated a hydrostatic valve that forced the charge downwards into the unit. As the valve moved, it compressed either the 40ft or the 80ft spring. The striker was held captive while the slide (see illustration on p. 45) moved. When the two bronze balls moved into line with a groove in the slide, the striker was released and struck the detonator. The detonator was embedded in four 9oz guncotton discs, which would explode after being initiated by the detonator. The D-type was far more accurate than previous weapons. Although the hydrostatically operated weapon was not perfected straightaway, it soon became clear that it was easier to deploy and far more reliable.

Gwynne's contribution to the project was the primer safety device, which held the primer away from the detonator by a spring-and-groove arrangement. Before dropping the depth charge, the safety fork was removed but the primer was locked in position, again by a ball-and-groove mechanism similar to that of the pistol. The end of the primer allowed water to flow in behind the extender sleeve plate and release the ball at the right pressure. This released the spindle, and the primer extended to contact with the detonator. This ingenious device allowed the depth charge to be safely handled at all times and it became dangerous only when it was immersed in water.

The marrying of these two ideas gave the navy a weapon with far greater offensive potential and a reliability it had not hitherto known. In his interview with the American patent office, Lieutenant Commander Herbert Octavius Mock RN expressed contempt for the old type of lanyard-operated depth charge, known as the Sperry depth charge, which was then still in use by the United States Navy. He said: 'I remember discussing the whole thing with Lieutenant Wilkinson, and that I thought it was very amateurish compared with what we had.'[3]

The model D was originally set to fire at depths of 40ft or 80ft, and it will be apparent that these were the operating depths claimed for the early A-, B- and C- lanyard-operated types. However it was far easier to lay a D-type – and far more certain that it would go off at the given depth – than one of A-, B- or C-type. There were two further depth charge types, the E- and F-, which operated on virtually the same principle, but the F-type was intended to be fired from a thrower. The D-type was released from laying gear, fixed to the deck, whose chief feature was a pair of rails that allowed the depth charge to be rolled off the side of the ship once the wire-hawser lashings had been released.

The F-type charge was considered to be worth a series of trials to establish how it would behave when fired from a bomb thrower and the *Redwing* was used to test the charge and bomb gun on 4 December 1915. The reliable *Redwing* was again out on trials on 9 and 10 December 1915, testing the F-type depth charge with a bomb gun to see if it was as effective as the D-type. The F-type had to have a 4ft-long stabilizing tail added to its after body and that part was placed in the gun barrel. In order to retrieve the weapon it was fitted with a pick-up wire and cork floats. Herbert Taylor and Lieutenant Courtis were present on the *Redwing* and the projectile was filled with sand and fitted with a pistol. The charge was tested at ranges between 50yd and 150yd at a depth of 35ft but with the pistol set at a 60ft depth. From this experiment they wanted to see if the pistol fired from the shock of being launched and hitting the water.

The explosive charge itself had to be detonated relatively close to the submarine. In the words of one officer at the time:

The Mark II depth-charge thrower ready to launch the Mark VII depth charge.

Contrary to popular belief, which credits a depth charge with being able to sink a submarine at a hundred yards or more, it was necessary to explode it within 14ft of a submarine to ensure destruction. Up to 28ft the explosion might be expected to disable a submarine to the extent of forcing her to the surface, where she could be rammed or sunk by gunfire; while up to 60ft the morale effect on the crew was considerable and might force the submarine to the surface.[4]

By 1924 the D-type depth charge had been in service for eight years and was used with the Mark IV pistol and the Mark V primer. The pistol itself had been found wanting when the depth charge was fired from a launcher. Taylor continued to work on other ideas for the pistol and one particularly came to the fore. This was an idea by which two separate diaphragms had to be moved in opposite directions to make the pistol fire. Only water pressure could do this and this would stop the depth charge from firing by inertia only. It required a reliable seal if it was to operate properly and the gland that provided the seal proved difficult to make watertight.

It was not until the two diaphragms were combined in one unit that this particular problem was solved, about 1930, and this led to development of the types of depth charge used in the Second World War. A leak hole allowed water

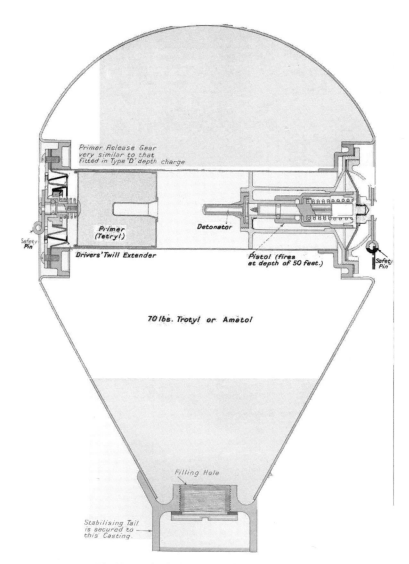

TYPE F DEPTH CHARGE.
SCALE HALF SIZE

Primer Release Gear
very similar to that
fitted in Type 'D' depth charge

Primer
(Tetryl)

Detonator

Safety
Pin

Drivers' Twill Extender

Pistol (fires
at depth of 50 feet.)

Safety
Pin

70 lbs. Trotyl or Amatol

Filling Hole

Stabilising Tail
is secured to —
this Casting.

The F-type depth charge, used from a bomb thrower.

into the area around the two bellows, which were forced apart as water was forced into the area at greater and greater depths. Gwynne's idea of a safety primer was then done away with, because in this case the primer was placed in position by hand before any action. This latest version of the pistol was called the Mark VII and went into service in 1935. When firing a five-charge pattern,

A bomb thrower on HMS Hyderabad *with F-type depth charge.* George Malcolmson Collection

the depth settings would be 50ft, 100ft, 150ft, 250ft, 300ft and 500ft. A primer of different design was required, and it also was called the Mark VII.

According to the Depth Charge Handbook of 1944 there were three main safety requirements of a depth charge. Two of them are obvious, in that the charge has to go off at the right depth and should not go off when the launching ship is in the vicinity. The final safety feature was more subtle: the depth charge had to be safe when subjected to unexpected water pressure. If the ship were sunk, this could set off all its charges when they reached the set depth. This same applied to an aircraft crashing in the sea if the depth charges were on board and also if charges were released into the sea by heavy weather or accident.[5] The new Mark VII pistol and depth charge were supposed to be safe in any of these situations.

The Mark VII depth charge was shaped like a drum, welded down the side, with a cover at each end. A steel tube passed through the centre and into this was placed the primer. There were three locating slots in the primer tube: two at one end, locating the pistol and depth adjuster, and one at the other end for the primer safety gear. The casing had three eyes welded to it, two at the pistol end and one at the other end. The main drum had two bungs at the primer end, so it could be filled with explosive. The pistol in the Mark VII relied on one of three actions to initiate firing: leakage, hydrostatic pressure and time. In the leak-hole type of pistol, water entered a chamber in the primer tube through an aperture and the rate of entry was controlled by the size of the hole, which was adjustable. The water pressure, increasing with depth, pushed apart two rods that were diametrically opposed, and this compressed a spring-loaded firing pin. Within the shaft of one rod were two captive ball bearings in a groove; the movement eventually let the balls leave the groove, releasing the spring and firing the pin at the right depth.

The rate at which a depth charge sank, the water pressure and rate of entry were all known and the pressure needed to force the two rods apart was a fixed value. The size of the water entry port controlled the depth setting. By revolving an orifice plate at the end of the pistol, a different hole moved into line with the water entry port, changing the depth setting. If the plate was turned further, the water ports were blocked and the depth charge was in safe mode. There was also a safety-firing rod, which prevented the two rods from being forced apart until a depth had been set on the depth-setting key.

In the Mark VII, the primer safety gear (where used) was kept apart from the detonator by the primer placer gear. This consisted of a primer, a cylindrical brass case filled with priming composition and an envelope or aperture where the detonator sat when ready. The whole thing was connected, through a bung in the end of the case, to a spindle with an annular groove in it. A spring, placed between the primer and the bung, compressed the primer onto the detonator. The spindle was held in place by a fork, which was attached to the ship's structure but placed on the annular groove. When the charge was released, the fork was pulled off, thus removing the safety feature. This clearly differed from Gwynne's idea and in the aircraft-launched versions there were no primer safety devices.

One other development was improvement of the shallow firing pistol, which was needed for inshore waters and was expected to operate at depths of 60ft to 280ft. This meant that its firing spring would be calibrated at 30ft. Extensive trials were carried out in the mud in Portsmouth Harbour and proved that problems might arise if the depth charge landed in mud. Taylor had certainly tested such devices by throwing them into the mud off Portsmouth, to see how they reacted. There were some failures, but the possibility that one or two might not function was accepted as a fact of life.

The main depth charge used by the Royal Navy in the Second World War was the Mark VII, introduced in 1935, fitted with the Mark VII pistol for use against submarines or the Mark VIII pistol for harbour defence. As with all military situations, old stock was pressed into service when not enough modern weapons were available, so the D-type depth charge with the Mark IV pistol was still in service in 1939.

There had been premature explosions of the shallow firing pistol on HMS *Mistletoe*, *Viola* and *Vivien* as early as 1918, and trials were carried out to establish why. It seems that the Mark IV pistol had design flaws, potentially fatal. Taylor and the team at the Mining School tested the pistols time and again; they found three main causes of failure:

1. Dropping the charge primer-end down from a height of over 40ft.
2. The striker rod being broken at the groove where the two captive balls were held.
3. Poor assembly of the ball-and-groove mechanism.

In the end the Mark V pistol was designed, for use exclusively in depth-charge throwers.

Problems remained with the ball-and-groove mechanism and the firing spring. In the trials following the problems in 1918, Taylor's team had found that when the pistol was assembled, the balls were sometimes not fitted properly into the groove and therefore the person assembling it was to blame. It may be this that was meant in comments on the pistols supplied from RNAD Priddy's Hard. When some Mark VIII pistols (introduced in 1935) were found not to fire, a new spring was decided upon for the firing mechanism. This spring led to the possibility of half-cocking when the pistol was calibrated, after which any external knock could set the firing striker off. If pistols had been left like that inside a ship, the consequences could have been disastrous. Altering the limit of the spring adjuster solved the problem in 1941, but it was thought much safer not to calibrate the pistols. Inevitably this meant pistols were less accurate than they should have been.

Types of British depth-charge pistols

Pistol	Purpose	Operating depth
I	Design model (prototype)	40–80ft
II	Design model (prototype)	40–80ft
III	Design model (prototype)	40–80ft
IV		
	Service model, 1915–39	
	(IV* and IV** had improved inertia qualities)	40–80ft
V	Designed exclusively for use from	
	depth-charge throwers	15–80ft
VI	Shallow firing, variable settings	
	(large dome with four depth settings on adjuster)	15–80ft
VII	No hydrostatic primer (primer was placed	
	before operation). Introduced 1935	50–500ft
VII*	Different manufacturing technique	50–500ft
VIII	Shallow firing for harbour defence	60–280ft

The depth charge in service

The depth charge was relatively easy to mount: the throwers could be fixed to the deck of a ship with just a few bolts, and the rails and traps could be fabricated in any engineering workshop. It was inevitable therefore that Britain's large merchant shipping fleet would be armed with the weapon in wartime. In the Second World War, the concept of the Defensively Equipped Merchant Ship was born and it seemed sensible to arm them with depth charges. It was soon found that many of these vessels required a special depth-

A Mark IV thrower at Thornycroft's Woolston works.

charge pistol because they were so slow. In April 1941 the pistols were modified so that they would not fire at depths of 50ft and 100ft, thereby removing the risk of a slow ship being blown up by its own charge. These pistols were marked with the suffix A after their mark, to identify them.

Drill

On board ship, the stern had two rail launchers, each with one depth charge. On the port and starboard sides, slightly forward of the stern, were the throwers, two on each side. During the Second World War these systems were

The depth-charge thrower production line at Woolston.

refined but, as mentioned, the old systems were still in use too. When operating a rail-mounted system, the officer of the quarterdeck normally checked the setting. He had a whistle and stopwatch, and was responsible for reloading.

Two men were detailed to operate the rail system, the number one and the number two. The process went like this: the number one removed the pistol covers and set the depths on them by moving an arm on the brass dial face. On the order 'Stand by' he removed the adjuster key from the depth charge and the safety pin from the trap. After reporting this, he simply stood by the release lever on the rails, ready to let the charges go.

The number two's responsibility was to take care of the primers. He secured the primer in the armed position, and connected up the Inglefield clips when the safety gear was in use. He was also responsible for checking that no foul-ups occurred with the charges and that, when reloading, new batches of charges were in position on the rails. The thing about the rail system was that it was simple and this is why escort captains were often reluctant to let it go, even when offered newer equipment. It required only two men to operate and, with the depth charge able to burst at varying depths, it could have a fair chance of hitting a target.

Using depth-charge throwers, the earliest service weapon being the Mark II, took five men. Numbers one to five had, as in the rail version, different responsibilities. The commander was the number one, who set the depth and fired the weapon. His role was virtually the same as the number one in the rail system. He withdrew the firing wedge when the thrower was ready and he was the person who removed the breechblock and inserted the firing cartridge, which was normally a small cordite charge.

The number two was the loading and priming number and, as with the rails, he was responsible for placing the primers. With the number three, he removed any securing wires and helped to handle the carrier into the thrower. His job was to install the primer, or clips if using the primer safety gear. The number three was there to lift and shift; he was required to help number two and worked on the hoists when reloading. Number four was responsible for the loading slings and tackle, and took care of the lifting gear. Number five was the assistant and effectively just helped the other numbers. Bearing in mind that each thrower launched one depth charge the advantages of using rails must be obvious. In a rough sea it was highly likely that throwers would incur casualties among their crews. But they did provide that vital extra range and accuracy.

At the beginning of the Second World War, there were two ways of indicating when to fire the throwers. The first was nothing more complex than a buzzer: when the number one heard the buzzer he fired the thrower. A more sophisticated system was used with Mark II and Mark IV throwers, both single-shot devices. A firing clock was used to fire the thrower and this normally included a lamp and a buzzer. The clock was meant to ensure that, when making an attack, the depth charges went over the side at even intervals,

The lightweight thrower's breech mechanism.

so that one would not have a counter-mining effect on another. The buzzer on the clock sounded a 3-second warning; when the lamp lit, the thrower was fired. The navy even required the clock itself to be started by the Anti-submarine Recorder type 144 or 145. The navy ordered at least 300 clocks of this type in May 1943 from two firms, PAM of Guildford and Mellers of Bromley.

The lightweight thrower being tested at Woolston works.

On the receiving end

How it felt to be on the receiving end has been dramatized in films, and Wolfgang Pederson's *Das Boot* gives a chilling interpretation of the effect of depth charges. The first U-boat to suffer a depth-charge attack was the U-68, commanded by Lothar Güntzel. It was lost on 22 March 1916 after an attack by a Q-ship, the *Farnborough*. In fact the U-boat was attacked first by gunfire from the *Farnborough*'s 12-pounder of 12 cwt guns and it was not until she began to sink that the U-boat was attacked with one, then two more depth charges.

The commander of U-49, on his return to Emden in May 1917, reported that he had been attacked by marine bombs and the confidence that U-boat crews had enjoyed up to that point was slightly rocked. The U-boat commander Speiss, who wrote on the subject, experienced an attack and found that he and his crew were forced into darkness and rocked around the seas. The motor boat *Salmon* attacked UC-7 on 6 July 1916 off Lowestoft. UC-7 was thought to have been sunk by depth charges, as later that year were UB-44 and, in December, UC-19.

However, it was difficult to know how much damage the boat had suffered or whether it had been destroyed. This was especially so when the submarines used the ruse of letting off oil and debris to suggest that they had been sunk. British crews were only too ready to accept this as evidence. The submarine

UC-44 was known to have done this by jettisoning wooden parts and fuel from her after torpedo tube in an attack on 15 February 1917.

There was also a strong question mark over the effect on crew morale after such attacks. When a new and untried weapon is used against an opponent, its effect is far more powerful than if such a weapon is known and trained for. Some German crews were found to have difficulty practising their drill on the days after a depth-charge attack. They were much poorer at carrying out their tasks and some clearly broke under the strain. The effect could be seen as cumulative and therefore the longer the depth charge was used, and the greater the quantity, the less German crews were able to maintain high morale. The main problem was the length of the attack. U-21, commanded by Lieutenant Hersing, was attacked off the coast of Ireland for five hours continuously. During the Second World War it was not unknown for attacks to last forty hours or more.

The depth charging of the British submarine J2 on 6 August 1917 was an interesting case of the effect of the depth charge on the crew. On passage to the Danish coast, she was sighted by light cruisers and torpedo boat destroyers and dived to avoid them. The captain knew at the time that there were allied forces in the area. The boat descended to about 90ft. The first depth charge exploded aft of the submarine and the men in the steering flat were lifted off their feet. A second depth charge exploded near the vessel and the crew stated they could clearly hear sweep wires passing through the water. Whether the boat was attacked by an explosive sweep is not clear. A third explosion occurred and the resulting damage was listed in the captain's report:

a) 7 containers in no. 4 battery leaking slightly (all these are in the same row).

b) Several cells in the batteries had their wooden separators shaken down causing shorts and low densities.

c) The deviation of the magnetic compasses underwent a permanent change of 5°.

d) Hack watch, which was in its box, had its regulator jammed hard to slow.

e) The lighting system was damaged so that only the police lights were kept on.

f) The helm jammed amidships at 90 feet but was quite free when we came to the surface again and gave no trouble …. The after hydroplanes worked very stiffly at 90 feet and were unworkable at 120 feet.[6]

As already mentioned, the effects on morale could be considerable and great emphasis is placed on the men looking to their officers to help them get through the depth-charge effects. Lieutenant Commander V M Cooper states:

Personally on this occasion I felt most uneasy, as it seemed to me that we were being given away by something as the depth charges appeared to be dropped with great accuracy. This was my second experience of being depth charged and on this occasion it was apparent, by means of hydrophone gear, that the enemy had a very good estimation of our position. I do not think that in the majority of cases there is any permanent morale effect; it might perhaps affect highly-strung individuals. It was noticed that for a day or two afterwards some men started on being woken from sleep or on being touched suddenly and unexpectedly by other persons.[7]

His view of the long-term effects is interesting, but it hides the fact that Cooper himself shortly left the submarine service because of these attacks. In his later career in the army he demonstrated considerable bravery and won the DSO.

In a further demonstration of British crews on the receiving end of the weapon, on 10 February 1918, Lieutenant Tweedy of HM Submarine D7 was viewing the trawler HMS *Pelican* through the periscope. When the submarine dived, the *Pelican* quickly attacked and let go three depth charges. The effect on the crew of the initial explosion was quite unsettling on its own but, according to the boat's log, 'Very shortly afterwards [there was] a second explosion. This was considerably more violent, shattering several lights and flooding the after periscope'.[8] This was a depth charge; and it was calculated that it exploded 150yd from the submarine.

Cases of mistaken identity such as this were not uncommon and so some British submariners were well aware of the powerful effects of the new depth-charge system. The British submarine L2 was also attacked, this time by American submarines, and had to dive to 356ft to escape her attackers. It is said that the depth charges used by the Americans exploded about 250ft above the submarine, but even so the commander reported that 'we proceeded to 200 feet at which depth an external ballast tank collapsed, and the boat sank stern first to depths we had no means of gauging. With the boat at an angle of 60°, the acid pouring from the batteries and squirts of water through joints in the hull'.

Even if no damage was sustained, the weapon was a terrible threat to submarine commanders, who had thought themselves safe under water. What did the U-boats make of the threat? When the U-29 was sunk on 13 December 1916 by two depth charges from HMS *Landrail* at 51°09′N, 1°46′E (south of the Goodwin Sands in the Strait of Dover), twenty-two crew died: all hands were lost. Many, many more boats were claimed and the experience was not one to be contemplated lightly.

The production of depth charges became critical to the anti-submarine war. In July 1917, for example, only 140 charges were being produced each week. At the beginning of 1917, ships were being allocated four depth charges, two D-type and two D*-type. Many vessels in the anti-submarine force were not supplied with charges at all. Admiral Sir John Jellicoe stated that 'During the greater part of the year 1917, however, it was only possible to supply destroyers with a small number of depth charges, which was their principal anti-submarine weapon; as it became feasible to increase largely the supply of these charges to destroyers, so the violence of the attack on the submarines increased, and their losses became heavier'.[9] By the end of 1917, output had risen to about 800 per week and the use of such weapons hovered between 200 and 300 a month. In comparison to this the last six months of 1918 saw 2,000 depth charges a month being used in action.

Before the Second World War, the main suppliers of ready-made depth charges were the Royal Naval Armaments Depot, Priddy's Hard, Gosport, and the main explosive-handling facility at Woolwich Arsenal. Cases and pistols were manufactured externally and then brought together at Priddy's Hard or Woolwich. Some depth charges were filled with explosive at Priddy's Hard, but much of this work was done under contract, by firms at Faversham and by Vickers at Banbury. The navy also had its own filling station at Gainsborough in Lincolnshire, specially for filling mines and sinkers – probably the sinker Mark I(M) – with TNT.

The Royal Naval Armament Depot of Priddy's Hard was fundamental to the supply of mines, depth charges and explosive paravanes. According to the Senior Armament Supply Officer,

> The explosive paravane was located at Priddy's Hard from its inception and later with its development into the protector paravane it was arranged, owing to the inability of the Naval Engineer Officer of the Dockyard to take over this work, that the whole work should be done at Priddy's Hard, pending the opening of a depot at Granton.[10]

The paravanes were delivered empty from various engineering firms and then filled with TNT at the site. They were also tested and repaired at the site and then special storage facility was prepared to accommodate them and their tools and boxes. He continues: 'some 13,000 square feet of surrounds was soon found insufficient for the service apart from anxiety always attendant.'[11] In fact the almost complete reliance on this site for the supply of paravanes meant that fifty-four staff were allocated to them. Ruston and Proctor, who made agricultural machinery, manufactured the paravanes.

The depth charge was accommodated at both Gunwharf and Priddy's Hard. The officer records that 'Later its development into the several types of depth charges also had to be provided for from Priddy's Hard as the centre of receipt, manipulation storage and distribution, the pistols and accessories being similarly dealt with at Gunwharf. ... In view of the large requirements a large storehouse for a stock of many thousands of depth charges with a room adjacent for examination and fitting up prior to issue and a storehouse for boxes were erected at Priddy's Hard and issue to the Fleet, made according to programme'.[12] This work coincided with a massive increase in the employment of women as munition workers. At Priddy's Hard there were 709 workers on the site.[13]

By 1918 the use of depth charges had become far more widespread, but the detection and sinking of enemy submarines was still a severe problem. Consider the experience of Lieutenant F Baker, commanding HMS *Loyal* on 20 March 1918, when he spotted the coastal minelayer UC-48 off the western end of the Isle of Wight. Baker's first reaction was, in his own words, to ram her. He then considered the idea of dropping depth charges in front of and behind the boat. UC submarines were capable of about $11\frac{1}{2}$ knots on the surface and about 7 knots submerged. Three charges were dropped but Baker complained that the port-side thrower did not discharge its projectile for some reason, though it had been correctly maintained. After several passes only some wooden debris was seen in the water and the crew had very little idea whether they had hit their target or not. This problem was to plague all anti-submarine commanders until they had efficient hydrophones.

The story of detection really forms part of another history, since in a book such as this there is not enough space to do it justice, but Britain had no effective submarine detection device at the beginning of the First World War. Detecting a U-boat was critical because the general gun-armed boat had such a short space of time to train her guns and fire. A U-boat might normally take 35 to 45 seconds to dive and completely disappear. A very well trained crew could crash-dive in 30 seconds. Detection underwater was essential.

The development of the hydrophone can be attributed to Commander C P Ryan at the Admiralty Experimental Station at Hawkcraig. The Admiralty began to develop the idea of listening to underwater sounds in 1915 by establishing listening stations. When Ryan had perfected the idea of the static hydrophone, about 400 were made and they were used at a depth of 50 to 100 fathoms (300–600ft). He also proposed a system using microphones to trigger mines, an idea that later took shape as a magnetophone that would register U-boats only when they were in the immediate vicinity of the listening device and therefore the mine. When listening stations became more developed and therefore more efficient, they did have some success in attacking U-boats. UB-29 was the first victim, off Cap Gris Nez on 20 April 1918. The auxiliary patrol, one of the main anti-submarine forces of the First World War, included 300 warships and some 4,000 auxiliaries, all of which utilized the hydrophone when it became available. Ryan was also responsible for another innovation, the drifter-type hydrophone set that could be used from a vessel to detect submarines.

From 1915 several different designs of hydrophone were being developed. One of the main problems was that in many cases the listening ship had to stop to listen for submarines. Both Ryan and a gentleman called G H Nash invented

Nash fish-type hydrophones being tested. George Malcolmson Collection

towed hydrophones, which were known as 'the fish'. These large units were towed behind the vessel and looked something like a torpedo (see illustrations above and below). The Admiralty ordered 136 complete sets. Ryan's version was similar to Nash's, but with the main unit encased in rubber and hence it was known as a 'rubber eel'. The range of Ryan's hydrophone was about 5 miles. Ryan's device was non-directional and so they were towed in pairs and the bearing of the submarine was calculated through a compensator.

The German Navy did not pursue listening devices to anything like the extent of the Royal Navy. Obviously they were using the submarine in an aggressive way and so their need was not as great. Even so they did have the hydrophone and in anti-submarine use it was normally used by dangling it over the side of the hunting vessel. Two types were used, one of which was a towed buoy. As with the British versions, it was better to stop and listen for the enemy.[14]

A selection of fish hydrophones for different operations. George Malcolmson Collection

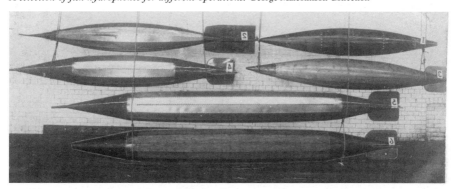

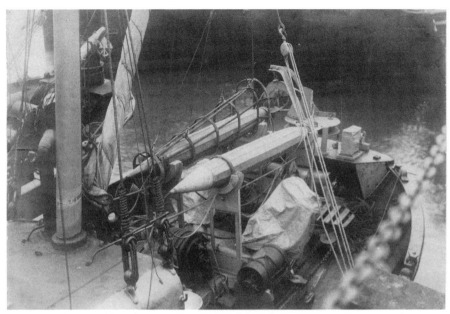

Nash hydrophones and launching apparatus on board ship. George Malcolmson Collection

Tactically the procedure was long-winded and required a great deal of energy and concentration. Three trawlers and a perhaps a P-boat would patrol a square of ocean 20 or 30 miles square. The trawlers formed a line-abreast formation and every fifteen minutes or so they would stop their engines and listen. Once a U-boat had been located, the detecting vessel would head for the

The stern of P-86, showing depth charges and paravane. George Malcolmson Collection

The rear of P-75 in wartime, showing how heavy the reliance on depth charges had become. She carries two rails and two throwers in the stern. The depth-charge arbors take up quite a lot of space on deck.
George Malcolmson Collection

boat and signal the position to the others. By 1917 hydrophones had developed so much so that motor launches were commonly equipped with them. They were also armed with depth charges, a pointer to the combined use of these two devices in the next war.

The effectiveness of these detection methods became clearer in 1918 and the question was largely resolved after an attack on 8 August 1918 by HMS *Opossum*. This destroyer and seven motor launches had detected the UC-49. They drifted with their engines off, since some of the vessels were equipped with hydrophones, and they listened for movement of the submarine under the water. The motor launches dropped charges on the area and then listened again. By this time the submarine was lying on the bottom with its engines switched off. When the submarine moved, they attacked her again. Finally the submarine was destroyed with depth charges and gunfire, and all the crew were lost. Better detection did not guarantee results, though. Admiral Sims wrote to Captain McCully of the US Navy:

> So far the difficulty has not been in getting contact with the enemy submarines but rather in attacking them successfully once contact is established. ... The dropping of a large number of depth charges in the vicinity of a submarine is a policy which has received my approval but which so far has not been productive of results. The average requirement of depth charges for the Queenstown Force

alone is about 1000 per month, and yet in spite of this very prodigal use of depth charges, no destroyer of the Queenstown Force is known to have sunk or seriously disabled an enemy submarine recently.[15]

When directional hydrophones were introduced, starting in 1917, the procedure that forced all the ships to stop and listen could be dropped. This did not noticeably improve the anti-submarine situation and it has been calculated that only four were actually destroyed by the use of hydrophone contact.[16]

Chapter Five

Mines and their complexities

Bump! Bump! Bump! Bump! We knew what it was, and painfully we waited for the crash that meant oblivion. It was phenomenal! The temporary inertia of us all was due to the peculiar behaviour of the mine. For such it was, and it seemed to continue for an eternity as the infernal engine of death bumped against the ship's side. In reality, the episode lasted only a few moments. Had the mine shattered the stillness of that cold, grey dawn with a detonation .... Immediately we left it astern, a Lewis gun and several rifles opened fire to perforate it and send it to where it would no longer be a menace to human life.[1]

This description of an unexploded mine demonstrates the terror that sailors had of hitting such a weapon; those who were unfortunate enough to detonate one were generally not around to tell the tale. This end result, the destruction of the enemy's shipping, was only achieved by mobilizing a large manufacturing capability and designing equipment so that mines would be reliable and safe for the user. For a mining campaign to have any chance of success, a great deal of work and thought was needed. It was estimated that during the First World War the Germans laid 43,636 mines worldwide, the British about 116,000 and the Americans 56,033.

Some mines float, some do not. The latter rest on the sea-bed and are called ground mines. Buoyant mines may be allowed to drift, but most are tethered to a 'sinker', which anchors them. Such mines contain a large air-space, usually around the explosive charge, and the length of the mooring cable is designed to make them float under the surface. The manufacture and use of mines are esoteric arts: they have long been seen as a weapon that requires a great deal of planning and special facilities. They have been used successfully to destroy surface ships and submarines and they were one of the greatest naval threats in both world wars. It is surprising therefore that mining is overlooked by many authors. It is

An interesting German postcard image, showing the use of mines and nets to stop submarine incursion.

perhaps the unglamorous nature of the work and the almost complete reliance on technology to carry out the final explosive act. Once the mines are laid, the naval authorities must rely on good manufacture and design to do their work. Mines have to be technically sound, because they cannot be repeatedly tested and, once laid, they cannot be altered in any way. The mine is an unconventional weapon, but when used in large numbers it has a deadly, crippling effect.

The author was once in discussion with a colleague who had experienced the full force of mines on Arctic convoys during the Second World War and was told that he saw a small warship, a Flower Class corvette, disappear before his eyes as the result of a mine explosion. Many unfortunate sailors and civilians met the same fate during the two world wars, but at their inception mines were not considered a weapon of much worth. There was something unwholesome about them: it was considered a lower sort of warfare that would use mines to sink ships.

In 1907 Admiral Lord Charles Beresford, Commander-in-Chief of the Home Fleet, had recommended that trawlers be used as minesweepers. Their widespread use in this role during the First World War gave their crews first-hand experience of mine warfare. In 1916 Chief Skipper Martin Fielding was minesweeping on the *Fair Maid* when the vessel was mined. He describes being knocked unconscious and waking up underwater:

> I felt as if my lungs would burst. I was trapped amongst wires and wreckage. I kicked and struggled and it seemed an eternity before I reached the surface. How far down I was I don't know, but it seemed a long way. On the surface men were screaming and shouting. The *Fair Maid* seemed to be about 100 yards away almost broken in two, but still upright and afloat.[2]

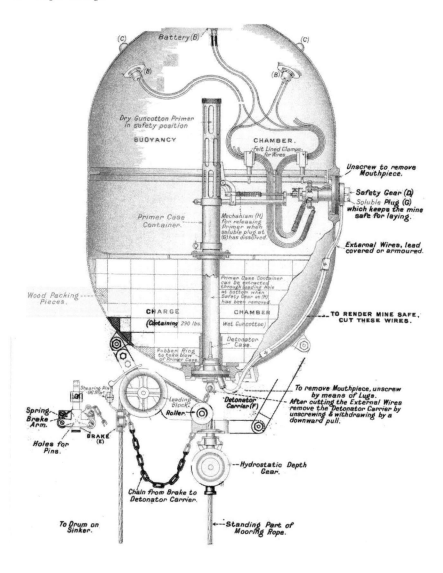

One of the German type II mines of the First World War.

   This seems a fairly typical experience for many men who were mined during the war, but mines didn't just affect sailors: they also affected civilians. Many mines were swept up onto lonely beaches, particularly in Ireland. Inquisitiveness could be very dangerous and on one occasion in Ireland nine men were killed by the explosion of a beached mine.

   There is no doubt that good use was made of mines in the First World War. One of the most successful mining campaigns was the Turkish mining of the

Dardanelles straits, which caused the allies very severe problems in 1915. One French battleship and three British capital ships suffered a similar fate to the *Audacious*. It is a well-known story – the Dardanelles naval campaign was a classic ships-*versus*-forts scenario – but the minefields were key to the whole Turkish defence. The allied fleet had to force the straits before troops could be landed at Gallipoli. The strategic significance of this was so great that, had the allies been successful, many now claim it could have ended the war much earlier, because this would have cut Turkey's links with Europe and probably prevented the Germans from supplying her. The main naval force had to silence the guns of a formidable row of fortresses on either side of the straits and deal with moveable land artillery.

First, though, the straits had to be swept by trawlers, for it was known that a significant minefield had been laid there. In fact the Turks had laid 373 mines between Keplez and Chanak. The subsequent minesweeping operation involved many escort ships and trawlers, under heavy gunfire from the coastal batteries. Preliminary minesweeping operations cleared the area where the fleet was to open its bombardment to within about 8,000yd (4½ miles) of the narrows. In addition, but unknown to the allies, on 8 March a Turkish vessel called the *Nousret* laid a small field of twenty mines in the area that Vice-Admiral Sackville H Carden had been bombarding previously. Four of these mines were found,

German Carbonit mines.

but the rest of this small group of mines caused havoc amongst the allied fleet. The French lost the *Bouvet* and the Royal Navy lost HMS *Inflexible*, HMS *Irresistible* and HMS *Ocean*. Both *Irresistible* and *Ocean* sank; the *Inflexible* had to go into dock for heavy repairs.

The mines that the Turks were using were of two main sorts. One was the German Carbonit mine, which was proving to be a useful weapon. The Turks, however, had developed another kind of mine using a float. It was spherical and was attached by a $^1/_2$-inch wire to a tin float filled with cork. The mine floated about 7ft below the surface. The firing method was ingenious in that it had a copper wire laid in wood around the edge of the tin. The wire had no contact with the tin unless a vessel hit the float, causing the copper to make a connection with the tin. This was enough to make a circuit with the internal batteries and thus blow the mine. This mine also incorporated a hydrostatic safety device and was rendered safe after 23 hours by a time clock. It may well have been this type of mine that caused the problems for the Royal Navy.

The strategic effect of using mines had many unexpected results. The British were very aware, possibly terrified, of them because of the severe effect they could have on the surface ships of the Royal Navy, which formed Britain's principal strategic naval weapon. To have built up a naval reputation over many years and then face the expectation of losing their capital ships to mines did not bear thinking about. Jellicoe stated that the Germans 'rely to a great extent on submarines, mines and torpedoes and will endeavour to make the fullest use of these'.[3] This hides the fact that Britain had long been experimenting with mines and HMS *Vernon* had been the centre of that work. But Britain had experimented with mines that were meant to destroy warships rather than submarines. This attitude might explain the fact that at the beginning of the war the navy was investing very little in the acquisition of mines. Submerged mines were developed, of course, but this was another sign of the myopia that saw surface vessels as the main threat. Nevertheless, great quantities of mines were laid during the first war, mainly to deny passage to the enemy. The main minefields laid between 1914 and 1918 were these:

Independent minefields in home waters
The Scarborough minefield off England's east coast is a good example.

Dover area minefields
The Dover command was one of the most important naval commands in Britain, since it was so close to continental Europe and controlled the passage from the North Sea to the Atlantic.

The Folkestone–Cap Gris Nez barrage
Admiral Bacon's idea in mining this area was to deny passage to U-boats along the shortest routes to their killing ground. The barrage was begun on 21

November 1917, using HII and HIV mines laid between 40ft and 100ft down. The field was extended 22 miles from Folkestone to Cap Gris Nez.

The Northern Barrage

This barrage, created by an agreement between the Americans and the British in December 1917, ran from the Orkney Islands to Bergen in Norway, in three separate sections. It was intended to restrict German submarines to the North Sea. The areas were sown with British HII mines and American Mark VI mines, some as much as 300ft down.

The Heligoland Bight minefields

After the Battle of Dogger Bank in 1915, the Germans laid 480 mines to trap vessels pursuing German ships into the Heligoland Bight. Britain also laid a minefield there and Jellicoe stated that its purpose was 'to lay mines so thoroughly in the Heligoland Bight as to force enemy submarines and other vessels to make their exits along Danish or Dutch coast in territorial waters. At the end of the exit we stationed submarines to signal enemy movements and to attack enemy vessels'.[4]

There were also several loop-controlled minefields around the British Isles, which relied upon a coil of cable laid on the sea-bed. These loops of cable were connected to a galvanometer on shore that would detect any large magnetic object passing over them; a string of mines could then be detonated. This system did cause an untimely exit for a number of U-boats and was thought to be relatively successful. Towards the end of the war, the allies even had some success in the Dardanelles, where shallow and deep minefields were laid to block the mouth of the strait. The Germans had given the Turks two cruisers: the *Breslau* and the *Goebben*. Both vessels attempted to leave for the Aegean Sea on 20 January 1918. It was a fatal mistake because both ships were mined, the *Breslau* being sunk and the *Goebben* damaged. Both sides therefore felt the effect of mines in the Dardanelles.

   The effect of a mine depends upon its distance from the target and the size of its explosive charge. For a given explosion at a specific distance from the target, the damage will be approximately proportional to the square root of the weight of the charge. This is tempered by the thickness of the ship's hull, the attitude of the ship at the time of firing, pressure waves generated by the explosive gaseous bubble and other varying factors. The buoyant mine was capable of operating at great depth in comparison to the later ground mine, which typically might use a 750lb charge in 10 fathoms (60ft) of water to cause serious damage to a ship.

   The earliest known naval mines in British service appeared about 1881. Two units were used, the 500lb naval mine and the 100lb service mine. The smaller one was an electro-contact mine and the larger was an observation mine. This limited stock of weapons would have to be augmented if Britain were to carry out a successful campaign. The Mining School was critical to the process of designing and servicing mines in the First World War. To return to Herbert Taylor, it is important to note that no real capacity for producing mines existed at the beginning of the war. Parts for 'design models' (prototypes) had to be made by the designers and then contracted out to a civilian manufacturer, who would produce the required item to the tolerances required. This reliance on industry could work well or badly depending on the abilities of any particular firm. The problem was enhanced by the fact that a lot of the equipment required by mines was specialized and often the staff had to be trained to produce the required fittings, thus slowing down the process.

In 1914 the Royal Navy's mining warfare programme had been based on board the old, floating HMS *Vernon*. By 1916 it was decided that the unit should be moved ashore and space at the Gunwharf site was made available. Rear Admiral Phipps Hornby was charged with moving the department and by December 1916 the Mining School was formed. Clearly, Taylor's view of its establishment was that he was responsible for the lion's share of the work. According to Poland's history of HMS *Vernon*, 'With ample space and a large new specialist staff concentrating wholly on the job and not distracted by diversions, a decisive improvement of Britain's mines now became a real possibility'.[5]

The Mining School became the place for the development and testing of mine equipment. Many different explosive mechanisms were developed in the period 1892–1913 and most were evaluated by HMS *Vernon*, including mines of these types:

- Vernon mine
- Sandford Oscillating mine
- Carbonit mine
- Vickers mine
- Harlé mine
- the acoustic mine (early form, not to be confused with A series)
- Léon torpedo mine

By 1915 the following mines were in use:

- Naval spherical Mark III
- Vickers Elia Mark IV to Mark VI
- Submarine Type S1 (designed to be fired from 21-inch torpedo tubes)

Probably a posed photograph of naval ratings with a British naval service mine. George Malcolmson Collection

- Submarine Type S2
- oscillating mines

In the First World War the mines used were almost all contact mines. In other words, the mine was fixed to a sinker or weight and sank below the surface, exploding on contact with a solid body. Britain had several pre-war designs in service during the early war months, in particular the Elia mine and the British service mine. The Elia mine, an Italian design, had been modified when it entered British service so that it was actuated by a mechanical device rather than an electrical one. This was because the glass phial used in the Hertz horn was sensitive to the shock of other mines in a field going off, so the Royal Navy preferred to use a long arm with a float on the end to operate the mine. There were three types: Mark Four, Mark Five and Mark Six. They all worked on the same principle. The rod safety sleeve and connector were held in the water via a cork float, which acted as a fin on the end of the rod. If the Elia mine was bumped, this gave it a rotary motion, which operated the detonator. This alteration did not prove successful and it was not until the H2 mine was introduced that the navy went back to the use of the Hertz horn.

British mines in 1914 were said to be very ineffective, since they relied on mechanical firing arms and were known to be woefully unreliable, so Carbonit mines were reluctantly purchased. At least one shipload of them – imported from Russia, but ironically designed in Germany – was used by British naval

A display of First World War explosive naval weaponry. The extra object on the extreme right is the HII mine and next to it is a D-type depth charge. The tall cylindrical objects on the left are oscillating mines. George Malcolmson Collection

forces. Carbonit mines had been evaluated by the Torpedo School at HMS *Vernon* and were reported in its annual publication of 1912. They had five firing horns in the upper half of the mine body. Mine rails were fitted to HMS *Niger* and the mines were tested in various ways. Although they were found to be far better at depth-keeping than British mines, there were negative comments about the size of the weapon and its ability to fire when struck by a ship. These comments may have been influenced by the fact that Carbonit charged £200 each for their weapons, whereas the British designs cost £40 each. HMS *Vernon* were of the opinion that German mines were of very inferior quality. This actually flies in the face of what we now know about British warship losses from hitting German mines.[6]

Captain Taprell Dorling, himself the commander of a destroyer minelayer, had this to say of British mines: 'In the course of experiments carried out during the war, only one-third of the old pattern British mines exploded on being struck by a target submarine. Of our stock of 20,000 in April 1917, only 1,500 were fit for laying.'[7] Yet Britain was not slow in developing new weapons. The school experimented with magnetic influence mines in the First World War. The M sinker, devised by the staff at *Vernon* and used off the Belgian coast, relied on the magnetic field cause by a passing vessel to move two needles that, when they touched, would blow up a 1,000lb charge of TNT. In the 1930s the British again experimented with magnetic mines, but it seems that the Germans first achieved the goal of manufacturing a magnetic influence mine

The two main types of early war mine: the Elia mine and the British service mine.

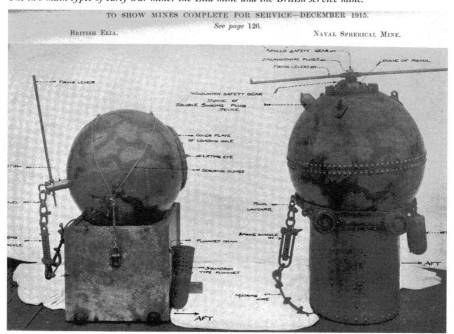

TO SHOW MINES COMPLETE FOR SERVICE—DECEMBER 1915.
See page 126.

that was safe, reliable, undetectable and – even more important – could be laid by aircraft.

Oscillating mines differed slightly from other types. They were expected to be used from destroyers and could vary their set depth by up to 4ft: they floated on the surface, then sank, then refloated again and were as much a terror weapon as a purely military one. The mine used a hydrostatic valve and an air vessel to alternately change its ballast state. This would happen every 25–40 seconds. An oscillating mine was an imperfect creature because its life was not very long and obviously it would drift with the tide. This sort of mine was controlled by the Geneva Convention but in the Second World War a similar idea, the drift mine, was widely used by all sides.

A drift mine was not tethered: it was left to drift in any direction until it came into contact with something and exploded. The key thing about it was that it had a limited life span. A drift mine was useful because it could be dropped into

A submarine-launched type III with its roller gear fitted.

SHOWING 2 METHODS OF CARRYING CRUISER MINES IN DRIFTERS & TRAWLERS

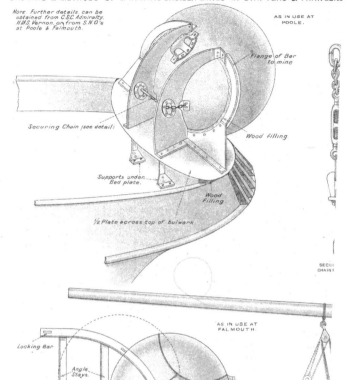

A drift mine as illustrated in the Annual Report of the Torpedo School in 1915. The mine is placed within the laying gear.

a harbour and allowed to float until it hit any enemy shipping anchored there. The Leon oscillating mine was adapted as a drift mine for this sort of use. In the Second World War a similar mine, the O Mark I, was thought to be an adaptation of this mine. Introduced in 1945, it was intended for use against small targets in enclosed areas such as harbours or river mouths.

A major transformation of the mine and sinker was the unified plummet-type submarine mine. It was invented by Robert Alexander Sturgeon, another engineer of the Mine Design Department. It consisted of a mine, sinker and plummet, or weight. When the mine was laid, these formed one body floating on the water. After a short time, the plummet was released and plummeted to the bottom. At a pre-determined depth, set by the length of the plummet line, the mine and sinker were unlocked. The sinker filled with water and gradually sank. When the plummet hit the sea-bed, it locked the mine cable; hence, when the sinker hit the sea-bed, it drew the mine under the surface. The mine then lay suspended under the surface, extended on a cable up to 1,000 fathoms (6,000ft) long. Depending on the type of firing mechanism, as a ship passed, it would brush the horns of the mine. The horns were part of an electrical circuit that exploded the main charge. Sturgeon's idea was very advanced because mines could be laid very quickly from the rear of a ship and were deposited in one piece at the required depth.

When it came to patenting the idea in 1916, Sturgeon, Alban Gwynne and Captain Skipworth of HMS *Vernon* applied for the patent jointly, though it would seem the idea was originally Sturgeon's. The automatic mine, which is described in much the same way as Sturgeon's idea, was known as early as 1902. The difference appears to be that in Sturgeon's design the mine and sinker stayed together on the surface while the minelayer travelled away from the laying area. The mine could then stabilize and sink without problems. It also meant that the mines could be laid more quickly and more accurately.

One other weapon of note should be mentioned: the American Mark VI mine. In April 1917 the Americans realized that they too had insufficient mines stockpiled for their war effort. The answer was provided by a civilian inventor, R C Browne of the L E Knott Apparatus Company of Cambridge, Massachusetts, and the idea was an antenna mine. It relied on the fact that a steel ship crossing a copper cable in salt water could produce a large enough electrical charge to actuate a mine. The copper antenna was attached to the top of the mine and a float kept it raised. The enemy submarine had only to touch the cable to set off the mine and this meant a far larger area of sea could be covered. The man who developed the idea for the US Navy was Simon P Fullinwider, of whom we have already heard. The Mark VI mine was born. The US Navy ordered 100,000 of these mines for the northern mine barrage in October 1917.

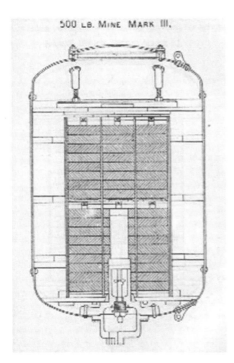

500 LB. MINE MARK III.

Britain was using the 500lb Mark III mine in 1914.

British mines produced in the First World War

Mine	Type	Charge	Operated by	Introduced
Mk III RE conversion	Buoyant	250lb guncotton	Contact	1914–15
Mk IV RE conversion	Buoyant	250lb guncotton	Contact	1914–15
Naval Spherical Mk I & II	Buoyant	250lb guncotton	Contact	1914–15
Naval Spherical Mk III	Buoyant	245lb guncotton	Contact	1914–15
Vickers Elia IV–VI [Mk VI: 125lb]	Buoyant	220lb TNT	Contact	1914–15
British Elia	Buoyant	220lb TNT	Contact	1914–15
S1 Type I	Non-buoyant, moored	125lb amatol	Contact	1915
S1 Type II	Non-buoyant, moored	220lb amatol	Contact	1915
Leon	Buoyant, unmoored	250lb amatol	Contact	1915
EC1 Net mine	Controlled and moored in net mesh	45lb TNT	Contact	1915
S Mk 3	Non-buoyant, moored	210lb amatol	Contact	1916
S4 & S4*	Non-buoyant, moored	210lb amatol	Contact	1916
H1	Buoyant, moored	250lb amatol	Contact	
H2	Buoyant, moored	320lb amatol	Contact	1917
H3	Buoyant, moored	40lb amatol	Contact	1917
Mine (M) sinker	Ground mine	1,000lb TNT	Magnetic	1917
H4	Buoyant, moored	150lb amatol	Contact	1917
EC2	Controlled and moored in net mesh	65lb amatol	Contact	1918
S Mk 5	Non-buoyant, moored	250lb amatol	Contact	1918

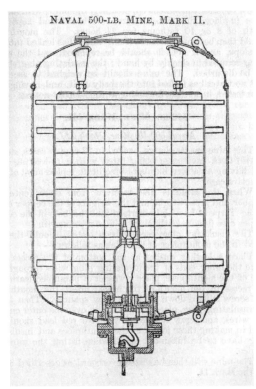

NAVAL 500-LB. MINE, MARK II.

The pre-war British Mark II mine.

This extensive list of mines was developed by a very small staff from 1915 onwards. As the war carried on, many more reserve officers were posted to the school and to *Vernon*, and many different projects could be carried out at once. Once it was realized that the unit was overflowing with people, ancillary activities were removed to other establishments.

Improvements in minesweeping
Burney's high-speed explosive sweep may not have been a great success as a weapon, but his idea also lent itself to minesweeping. The paravane was adapted so that it had a torpedo-shaped body, with a plane across its nose, and could be towed from the bow of a ship. It could be set so that, when towed, it would remain at a certain depth and always veer away from the ship. The mine-destructor paravane was not filled with explosive; instead, the head was fitted with steel jaws, intended to cut the cables of mines. Any ship could be fitted with this device and it gave a high degree of protection. According to a naval officer at the time, 'Within the limits of the wedge [formed by the two towing cables] the towing wire catches the mooring wire of a mine, the mine is deflected away from the ship, and the mooring wire slides into the jaws of the cutter by which it is severed'.[8] The maximum length of towing wire was about 110ft either side.

This idea was adapted for naval ships and merchant ships; the latter version was made by Vickers and known as the otter. In a similar way the paravane was used to carry out high-speed sweeps from the rear quarters of destroyers. This arrangement required a span of cable at the stern, held beneath the water by a separate depressor paravane. It enabled the two paravanes attached to long cables to be kept at depth and, as the name suggests, could be used at very high speeds. The anti-mine paravane was fitted to HMS *Melampus* and first tested on 4 November 1915. By February 1916 the Commander of the Paravane Department and Burney had convinced Admiral of the Fleet Lord Jellicoe at Scapa Flow that their system would be able to offset the appalling losses to mines that British shipping was suffering at that time. The tests worked and the way was open to produce them for the navy.

A Mark II depth-charge thrower on the deck of HMS Whitehall. George Malcolmson Collection

A minesweeping paravane designed by Burney. Note the jaws for cutting the sweep, above the nose.
George Malcolmson Collection

How effective was it? Well, if the explosive paravane was anything to go by, perhaps no great success might be expected, but it was believed that sixty-eight warships had cut mine cables with the paravane, representing a very significant tonnage saved, since among them were seven battleships and two battle cruisers. The commercial version, the otter, was thought to have saved 240,078 tons of merchant shipping.[9]

A minesweeping paravane on HMS Benbow. George Malcolmson Collection

By the end of the First World War the paravane was being used to sweep for mines. Herbert Taylor and F Pickford, the Principal Technical Officer of the period, jointly designed a 'paravane antidote'. This counter-measure, fitted between the mine and its mooring, made use of the overload-pull set-up on the mooring spindle. It was used to make an electrical contact to explode the mine, and so destroy the paravane, when its sweep wire met the mine's mooring rope. There was no other way of exploding the mine on contact with the sweep wire, but it was not clear if this system was adopted only because spending in this area was limited at the time.

In the Second World War, it was the Oropesa sweep that accounted for many mines. This device was a massive improvement in the navy's ability to sweep for mines, because it required only one vessel. The Oropesa was developed from the paravane, which in turn was developed for the Royal Navy from the ideas of Lieutenant C Dennis Burney, who invented the explosive sweep.

After the First World War
At the end of The First World War, the facilities at Gunwharf in Portsmouth Dockyard had been outstripped by the needs of mine warfare. The requirement for a new depot to service mines was established by a meeting at the Admiralty, at which the recommendations of various officers were taken into account. So was born the Mining Depot at Frater, not far from the Royal Naval Armaments Depot at Priddy's Hard in Gosport. Frater lay between Gosport and Fareham. The Royal Marine Engineers carried out the construction work and by 1919 many of the main buildings had been erected. At this time there were about twelve staff dealing with mines and sinkers recovered during the First World War.

In 1935, Frater came under the command of the Superintending Armament Supply Officer (SASO) at Priddy's Hard. The site at Frater employed fitters, turners, tinsmiths, joiners and electricians. Laboratory staff examined mines and their explosives, removed to a safe place. Once a mine was declared free of explosive, its detonators, clocks and workings could be examined by staff. It is clear from this that mines were not left on the shelves; they had constantly to be examined, repaired or modified, and reassembled.

During the war, no facilities were specifically designed for the storage or repair of mines; they were added on an ad hoc basis. By 1918 there were depots at Dover, Portsmouth, Plymouth, Woolwich, Wrabness (near Harwich), Immingham, Grangemouth and Inverness, and one on Malta. The laying capacity at the start of the war was 700 mines, whereas at the end of the war it was about 60,000 mines. In that time 131,313 had been laid and there were 106 minelayers of various sizes.[10] Considering the size of the operation in 1918, the work carried out by the experimental mining school was nothing short of Herculean. But the unreliability of British mines and their sinkers, along with the demand for larger quantities of mines, meant that a new establishment was needed.

By 1935 a civilian was in charge of the Frater site as Armament Supply Officer. The demand for mines became overwhelming by the time of the Second World War, and it was Frater that dealt with most of them. Hence the great changes and expansion that had taken place in the first war were, in time, directly beneficial by providing facilities for the second. The Admiralty's preparations had borne fruit.

In the Second World War, allied merchant shipping losses from mines amounted to 1,406,037 tons. By July 1939, an airborne magnetic mine was available, as well as the moored type. The British magnetic mine was the M Mark I. In this mine, a mu-metal rod bound with copper wire (forming a coil) extended through the mine, with end plates acting as intensifiers. Any movement of the coil that caused it to intersect lines of the earth's magnetic field or any change in field of the mine – typically caused by movement of a large body of iron, such as a ship – would generate an electro-motive force in the coil. This would be enough to operate a relay and therefore explode the mine. This principle also held good for ground mines, but the M Mark I was a buoyant weapon.

Mines were, by the early twentieth century, mainly reliant upon electrical circuits to fire them. The Hertz horn was the electrical device widely used, but it soon became apparent that all sorts of electrical devices could be incorporated into mines to enable them to perform different tasks. The evolution of electrical mining circuits could fill a separate work, but here I can only describe some of the more important changes in the technology of mines, if only to understand the impact that people like Herbert Taylor had on their development.

Mine components were as critical to the mining programme during the two world wars as the final weapon. They had to be constantly upgraded to confuse and baffle the enemy. Among the many devices used in mining circuits were the following:

- A/C (anti-countermining) switch – to stop a magnetic mine being set off by mechanical shock;
- amplifier – to amplify a signal in an acoustic mine where the detected signal level is low;
- battery – normally used to fire a detonator, but could also run supplementary circuits, such as clocks and delays;
- circuit breaker – switch used to isolate some electrical circuits or to render a mine safe;
- clock – set to flood a mine, thus making it useless, or to release a mine from its sinker, or even to arm a mine after a certain delay;
- condenser (capacitor) – used to put delay into an electrical circuit, for example to stop a mine reacting to a magnetic sweep, but enabling it to explode when a ship passes over;
- CR (coiled rod) unit – magnetic detection device, by which a metal ship's hull induced an electric current in two coils wound round a mu-metal rod, setting off a firing sequence;

- dashpot – an oil-filled pot that delayed operation of a firing switch, usually for safety;
- detector – first element of a firing circuit: a CR unit, acoustic vibrator or pressure unit;
- detonator – usually electrically operated, a device to set off a mine via the primer;
- detonator release – similar to the primer safety device, it kept the detonator away from the primer until the mine was activated;
- electrolytic switch – developed in the 1930s and more accurate than clockwork, this timer could activate or deactivate circuits after 7–42 days;
- flooder – could be fitted to a buoyant mine to flood and sink it and so control its lifespan;
- hydrostatic switch – operated by water pressure, usually set to stop a mine exploding except at its intended depth; protected surface ships against anti-submarine mines;
- mooring switch – to isolate detonator or battery while mooring cable was under tension;
- pressure unit – a single-pole switch operated by a water jet, created by the small difference in water pressure on the sea-bed caused by passage of a ship overhead;
- relay – a very sensitive switch operated by electric current (just 5 microamps in some cases) induced into a coil, often used with CR rod or vibrator to detonate a mine, it had to resist the shock of being thrown about – a critical component in air-launched weapons;
- sterilizer – often a clock or switch, this rendered a mine harmless (like a flooder);
- vibrator – sound detector in acoustic mines, set off by sound waves travelling through the water, making contacts on the vibrator open and shut, thus making an electrical circuit.

Having glanced at the multiplicity of electrical systems used in mines, it is time to look at the inventions of Herbert Taylor that improved British mining. The introduction of the CR rod was one of the most important changes in the magnetic ground mine; Taylor worked on several types of relay that could be used with such a mine. Some of his ideas were incorporated into a mine design that utilized the CR rod and eventually became the M Mark I. Taylor produced more sensitive relays.

The E-type was invented by Taylor and a Mr P Cozens, who was a draughtsman at the establishment. Previous designs were not able to function reliably with the very low currents required. The E-type prompted the comment from the Admiralty: 'This comprises a radical departure from any known relays.' Once the tests were complete it was expected to be used in all magnetic mine versions. The Admiralty expected to order large quantities and

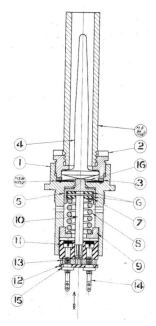

Taylor's redesigned switch horn.

so was putting its faith in Taylor's and Cozens' ideas. A second relay, the F-type, used improved magnetic materials and provided a magnet of a particular form to give high magnetic density. The third type of relay invented was designed to fire on a falling voltage. It was used for non-contact mines and was intended to delay the firing of a mine until it reached the optimal position under the target ship. This was a further collaboration of Cozens and Taylor, with the assistance this time of the Chief Technical Adviser, F B Shaw, and the Senior Technical Officer, C B Johnson.

According to the author Arthur Ingham, an authority on mining, Taylor's invention of the electrically operated switch horn meant that Britain possessed one of the most sensitive mines produced by any military power before the Second World War. Taylor came up with the idea of the switch horn in 1930. This might not seem like a critical piece of equipment, but it was the final point of contact between the explosive device and ship. It needed only one central battery, whereas a Hertz horn had to have a battery for each horn. Taylor's design thus improved reliability and also overthrew previous thinking, because the Hertz horn did not become an active electrical cell until an enemy ship struck it, which meant there was no question of running the battery flat. Improvements in dry batteries meant that a switch horn was now a viable alternative.

Effectively it consisted of an exposed spike, whose inner end formed a mushroom head held against a heavily loaded spring. Between the head and the inner electrical contact was a metal diaphragm, and the whole thing was arranged so that any movement of the horn would detonate the mine. The Mark XV mine was the first to employ this type of horn. It was incorporated into the design of the earlier Mark XIV mine to produce the Mark XVII, which was still in use at the start of the twenty-first century, demonstrating the worth of the design. At least 22,000 horns were made.

The flooder was another of his designs that became widely used. This consisted of a clock and a fuze assembly. When the clock was required to flood the mine, it activated a fuze that punctured a hole in the mine casing, thus allowing water in. Before this, soluble plugs had been used; when several mines exploded prematurely, it was found that some of the plugs had not been reliable. As the report said on the subject: 'There was no flooding available for all the required periods until the present design was evolved.'[11]

We have already discussed Taylor's improvement of the mine horn, but he and other members of the Mine Design Department also developed new

Taylor's mine clock and relay.

accessories for counter-mining purposes. One special unit consisted of an arm – suspended in a similar manner to Taylor's relay patent – bearing on a contact, which was securely mounted in the body of a unit and was retained in position by a small permanent magnet. When it was fixed in a mine, any shock imparted to the unit caused the arm to separate from the contact. Inertia caused a short delay during the remake of the circuit. Because of the relative lightness and sensitivity of the arm, this separation occurred just before the electro–motive force was generated in the coil unit, so the circuit was broken long enough to stop the mine from operating.

Counter-mining devices such as this were vital for non-contact mines; this one was used with the magnetic M Mark I mine. It was a collaborative effort with the Senior Technical Officer, Mr Johnson, and the Foreman, Mr Rigby, then working at the Mine Design Department. It is important to stress here that all Taylor's ideas – whether on his own or in collaboration with other people – were recognized by the Admiralty as having also reduced the cost of manufacture, apart from any other benefits.

As well as electrical equipment, there were also mechanical devices associated with the art of mining. The enemy's counter-measures could prevent the successful explosion of the mine, so the designer had to subvert them. If the mine was tethered, the enemy would try to cut its cable with a serrated sweeping wire – on which one strand stood out, making the wire 'serrated' – but there were devices to combat this, usually by cutting the sweep wire or diverting it away from the mine cable. One of the most ingenious was the sprocket. This was a spoked steel wheel, captured within a bracket fixed in line with the mine mooring cable. As the sweep wire passed along the cable, it encountered the wheel. This was finely made and revolved easily, allowing the sweep wire to pass through it, leaving the mooring cable untouched. This

Taylor's mine sinker.

device is thought to have been devised in 1911 by Assistant Paymaster C Bucknell.[12]

A later type of counter-measure, with a similar function to the sprocket, was the obstructor. This was a float moored at a pre-determined depth within a minefield and carrying an anti-sweeping device – a number of cutters in its mooring rope. It was laid by means of a sinker, a wheeled base carrying a tube in which the obstructor was stowed. When deployed, the float held up the cable

Taylor's anti-mining switch.

with the cutters on it. The cutters had two nickel-chromium blades with sharp, serrated teeth mounted at a small angle. When the sweeping wire encountered the obstructor, it was likely to get trapped between the cutters and eventually cut by one of them. This might not seem a great problem, but if a minesweeper lost a paravane it could be out of action for a long time while waiting for a replacement to be fitted. Obstructors were laid within minefields, starting in 1942, and were immediately effective.

The final counter-measure was the grapnel, three hooked prongs on a central fixture attached to the mine's mooring cable. When the cable was swept, the sweep would run into the jaws of the grapnel and either the sweep wire would break (even thick wires could easily be cut with a small force) or the grapnel would hook onto the sweep, which then dragged the mine with it. If it swept a second mine, this would explode and endanger the minesweeper.

Another mechanical device that Taylor developed was the mine sinker. This was effectively a carriage for a mine, which allowed it to be laid from rails. It anchored the mine on the sea-bed, so the mine stayed put and floated at a pre-determined depth. By the end of the Second World War, depth-taking could be achieved by one of four methods: plummet, hydrostat, float and fixed mooring. When designing such devices, the weight of the unit was of great importance because the sinker had to moor the mine at the right depth, but not allow it to be dragged along by strong sea currents.

Obviously, the life of the mooring and the laying facilities had to be considered, so the sinker was seen as an important component in a mine. Before

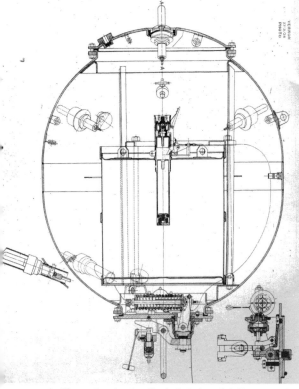

An illustration showing Taylor's design of shell construction.

the First World War, the Mark 6 and 7 sinkers were in use. Their maximum depth was 45 fathoms (270ft), whereas the Mark 8 – which became standard for H2 and H2* mines – could operate at anything from 60 to 200 fathoms (360–1,200ft). The version that most concerns us here is the Mark 14, designed by Herbert Taylor and introduced in 1933, which was basically an advance on the Mark 8 design. Its main feature was the dropping wheel, which would clamp the plummet cable when enough of it had been paid out. The Mark 14 could operate at depths of 100–1,000 fathoms (600–6,000ft), a massive increase on earlier mines. The greater depth was achieved by fitting a drum containing 100–200 fathoms of wire, or 500 fathoms or 1,000 fathoms (600–1,200ft, 3,000ft or 6,000ft).

Probably Taylor's greatest contribution in the field of mine sinkers was the Mark 16 submarine-laid sinker, introduced in 1934 and used until 1945. The Mark 16 sinker incorporated a loose bight pawl and a special case that could be rapidly drained or filled with water to aid the submarine's trim. A loose bight pawl was used on mines laid by submarines, to ensure that the mine never showed above the surface and did not get to its set depth until the submarine was well away. The complete mine unit fell to the sea-bed, where the positive buoyancy of the mine tended to pull it away from the sinker, at first delayed by some kind of device. When the mine rose, a hydrostat released a length of chain to form part of the mooring cable. The chain momentarily slackened the tension of the mooring cable, operating a locking mechanism on the sinker and stopping the rising mine under the surface. This was done by pawl and ratchet connected to the drum of the mooring cable; the chain therefore was known as a loose bight. These clever mechanical devices are simple yet effective and even in the late 1940s were used for standard submarine minelaying techniques.

Also in 1934 Taylor designed the Mark XVI mine for laying with the Mark 16 sinker. This was actually designed for use with the new minelaying submarines of

British minelaying submarine about to be launched. George Malcolmson Collection

the Porpoise class, fitted with chain conveyor gear. The new mines had ten horns and could be laid in 80–100 fathoms (480–600ft) of water. The charge was 320lb and they were designed for offensive laying purposes. The Mark XIV, introduced in 1933, was a development of the H2 with Hertz horns. It was 40in in diameter and had a detachable charge case containing either 320lb or 500lb of explosive. A larger, more buoyant mine, the Mark XV, was designed to maintain the taut cable at depths of 500ft and 1,000ft. Both Taylor's moored contact mines, the Mark XIV and Mark XV, became the standard Royal Navy mines of this type. When equipped with the new mine horn, the Mark XIV became the Mark XVII.

All these designs show the considerable contribution Herbert Taylor made, not only to the invention and development of the depth charge, but also in submarine mining. Over a period of twenty years he designed weapons that enabled the Royal Navy to enter the Second World War with an effective mining capability. During that war, 17,500 mines were laid by British surface ships and these damaged 174 German ships, of which 50 were repairable. The 3,000 mines laid by submarines damaged 67 vessels, of which only 8 were repairable. By far the most effective were the 55,000 mines laid by air: 1,347 vessels were damaged by these mines and 483 were repairable. Altogether, 1,047 German vessels were destroyed by mines and 1,588 were put out of action.

As a measure of the efficiency of the mine as a naval weapon, we can see that one vessel was damaged for every 47 mines laid. There was a downside to this; at least four submarines and fifteen surface ships were sunk while laying mines.[13] Compared to the First World War, when Britain laid 114,000 mines and sank 129 of the ships of the Central Powers, it is obvious that the destructive capability of mines had increased enormously by the end of the Second World War.

Chapter Six
Underwater weapons in other navies

The efficiency and effectiveness with which the German submarines waged war in the two world wars tends to hide the fact that Germany was as much in the dark as Britain was about what to do with submarines in the First World War. Germany's allies complicated the matter. Austria-Hungary and Turkey took responsibility for guarding certain waters and this meant that the anti-submarine techniques varied from one area of conflict to another. Like the British amongst their allies, the Germans led the way in developing weapons to counter submarines. These tended to take three forms: the depth charge, the explosive sweep and the mine.

In 1916 a secret British report detailed the methods the Germans were using against submarines at that time: steel wire nets, depth charges and submarine kites. The kites and nets were used in combination. The towed submarine kites were 6,560ft long and 46–52ft deep. The method of use was to literally try to catch a submarine in the net, which, although it sounds impossible, was why the nets were made to be able to withstand the force of a submarine entering them.[1] The idea was to have a formation of trawlers towing these nets in line ahead, but with each vessel slightly overlapping the net of the one ahead. This method was laborious and required large amounts of manpower and time to deploy. The nets were about 12ft mesh made of 1½in wire rope, with a head rope and foot rope of about 3in wire. The nets were gargantuan, about 16½ miles long, and they were usually intended to deny entry to harbours or river mouths.

German depth charges were very simple. The main version, introduced in 1915, was the C15, which was, to all intents and purposes, similar to the early British A-, B- and C-types in that it had a float, a lanyard and an explosive case. As with the British versions, the length of the lanyard determined the depth at which it would explode. Throwing it into the water started the whole mechanism: the depth charge sank, while the float remained on the surface. When the depth charge reached the end of the lanyard, it pulled a pin from the pistol, exploding the charge. This inefficient weapon left the Germans quite a long way behind the development of hydrostatically-operated devices. The Carbonit Company manufactured the C15 and many other mines for the German navy.[2]

Germany also utilized explosive sweeps: the *spenganchor* and the UD device. The former was a grappling iron attached to a kite, which was towed along at a certain depth (up to 30ft). The target submarine was meant to be grappled by the hook, which then dragged an explosive charge off the deck of one of the two towing vessels. The failure of the *spenganchor* design was that it relied on a time delay to explode the charge, rather than a hydrostatic device. The UD device was a towed device, electrically operated and not dissimilar to the Burney sweep in theory – and in practice, since it seems to have been relatively ineffective.[3]

German use of mines

In the First World War, the Germans laid mines in different ways, from different vessels and for several reasons. These were summed up by the Torpedo School at HMS *Vernon*. German minelayers laid long lines of mines in a pre-arranged barrage; the intention was

- to harass British trade and
- to inhibit the movement of fleets.

German submarines laid small groups of mines off British ports

- to cut off supplies from overseas and
- to damage seafarers' morale.

German warships, typically light cruisers and destroyers, laid mines at sea

- as a tactical measure during a fleet or cruiser action, or
- as part of an operation.[4]

The German Navy used four principal types of mine, known in British parlance at that time as types I–IV:

type I   carried 180lb of wet guncotton, total weight 560lb, 31½in diameter, dry guncotton primer, Hertz horn operated;

type II   carried 290lb of wet guncotton, total weight 710lb, 31½in diameter, more powerful cylindrical primer, Hertz horn operated;

type III carried 220lb of cast TNT, total weight 620lb, 34in diameter, cylindrical primer containing tetryl, Hertz horn operated;

type IV carried 180lb of wet guncotton, total weight 620lb, 34in diameter, cylindrical primer containing tetryl, Hertz horn operated.

Another view of the high-buoyancy type II mine laid by the Möwe *and swept by British trawlers.*

German mines were always laid with the sinker, which sank to the bottom of the sea. The mine was then released on its mooring cable to the correct depth. Just underneath the mine was a hydrostat, normally set to the correct depth before the mine was laid. When the mine had risen from the sea-bed, the

Loading a type II mine on board a German UC boat. George Malcolmson Collection

hydrostat, detecting the set water pressure, gripped the cable and this kept the mine at the right depth below the surface. The sinker, which was standard on all four types of mine, held up to 55 fathoms (330ft) of coiled mooring wire, which meant it could not be laid any deeper than 28 fathoms (168ft). The type IV was the mine most often laid by German UC submarines and for this application it used a specialized sinker, which had additional roller ways attached to it for release from the submarine.

Germany aggressively used mines against the British by laying minefields in river estuaries, where shipping would have to enter or exit, and around major ports. To aid in doing this, the Germans quickly developed the submarine minelayer. This was a major advance in tactics because of the hidden nature of the submarine, which was far more likely to be able to creep up to an enemy port unseen and lay a screen of mines without being attacked. The problem was that it was a very dangerous business and several submarines were lost during these minelaying activities. The UC boats, as they were known, were able to lay eighteen – later thirty-four – type IV mines from six vertical tubes.

How was it done? The mines were loaded via watertight hatchways in the deck and stored in a stern compartment. If we imagine two rows of mines in the stern, each mine was placed between guide rails fitted with rollers and then moved to a short expulsion chamber, which acted like a sea lock, with hatches on the inside and outside. The mine was placed in the chamber and the inner hatch closed. The outer door was then opened, to lay the mine. Compressed air was used to push the mine out into the sea. Because mines are heavy items they had to be compensated for when expelled. This meant taking on an equivalent amount of seawater to trim the submarine. German mines were arranged so

The German minelaying submarine UC-5 being towed in a heavy sea. George Malcolmson Collection

that they hit the sea-bed and then extended the explosive part from the sinker to the required depth.

What was it like when these mines went off? The commanding officer of the *Alyssum*, a naval sloop, describes it:

> Our particular mine must have caught us just under the bridge. All I remember about it was an appalling shock, and looking up into the air to find it full of brickbats and wondering if any were coming my way. As soon as I collected my wits, I looked round to find my navigator and first lieutenant on the deck beside me. One poor fellow had been blown clean off the bridge, and we found him trying to drag himself along the boat deck with his hands, both his legs being broken. Our foremost 4.7 gun and mounting were lifted clean out of the pedestal and were lying across the forecastle.[5]

The *Alyssum* was blown up on 18 March 1917.

Germany developed far more deadly weapons under the auspices of the Third Reich, and the whole perspective of the battle of scientific minds changed with Britain's entry into the Second World War. Germany set up mine warfare research establishments in 1920 and experimented with all sorts of methods of laying mines in the 1930s. In 1931, parachute mines were tested from aircraft but large stocks were never achieved before the Second World War. As a result only 470 were laid in the first three months of the war. The aerial-laid magnetic and acoustic mine were developed and put to use by Germany before Britain was able to do so. According to one modern author the Germans had begun to lay their magnetic and acoustic mine stocks before they had sufficient stores of such weapons. This mistake may have lost the Germans their opportunity to halt British shipping in 1940.[6]

Germany carried out one of the most successful mining campaigns of the Second World War, against the Russians. At Cape Juminda, off the Gulf of Finland, they laid just under 3,000 mines, which caught Soviet forces retreating from Tallinn. It was calculated that, during the evacuation from Tallinn to Leningrad, 25 of 29 larger transports were lost. The Soviet Baltic fleet lost five destroyers, two corvettes, two submarines and two patrol boats. During this action Finnish patrol boats sank one sailing ship and captured two tugs.

The German moored mines, like everyone else's, consisted of new designs and old ones. Interestingly, they never developed the use of the switch horn as widely as the British did. Most German contact mines were fitted with the Hertz horn. In the Second World War German mines were categorized by HMS *Vernon* on the basis of the known types (it seems there was no F or W type):

A – LMA air-dropped magnetic mine with 550kg charge;
B – LMB air-dropped magnetic mine with 960kg charge;

C – modified LMB;

D – modified LMA with altered acoustic or magnetic–acoustic firing;

E – booby-trap mine used in 1940;

G – air-dropped mine with 1,000kg charge, could be magnetic or acoustic;

H – RMA hemispheric ground magnetic mine, laid by surface craft;

I – RMH wooden ground mine, ship laid;

J – spherical mine with 12kg charge, suitable for beach and river applications;

K – KMA concrete mine with 75kg charge, mainly for coastal defence;

L – moored contact mine with 110kg charge;

M – BMC air-dropped contact mine;

N – TMC enlarged ground-influence mine with 900kg charge, magnetic or acoustic influence;

O – moored mine with 350kg charge, laid from vertical tubes on some U-boats;

P – LMF moored influence mine with 1,050kg charge;

Q – FMC shallow-water contact mine with 40kg charge, for beach defence;

R – UMB moored contact mine with 40kg charge and eight horns;

S – TMB submarine-laid mine with 500kg charge;

T – TMA magnetic mine, not used after 1941;

U – EMA oval moored contact mine with 150kg charge;

V – antenna mine;

X – EMD spherical moored contact mine with 150kg charge;

Y – EMC spherical moored contact mine with 300kg charge;

Z – UMA anti-submarine moored mine with 30kg charge.[7]

Mining in Germany had been greatly improved by the establishment of a mine warfare command in 1920. During the Second World War, mines used contact, antenna, magnetic or a combination of influences to detonate. The term 'antenna mine' deserves some explanation. An antenna mine consists of a mine tethered to a sinker, and with a float extended on a cable above the mine case. The long cable behaves like one side of an electrical circuit. If the submarine passes the antenna and touches it, this makes an electrical circuit inside the mine and explodes it.

German use of mines was not as successful as had been hoped, especially in view of the amount of naval action. For example, in the English Channel only two submarines were lost and only one of those, HMS *Swordfish*, is thought to have been mined. She was sunk on 7 November 1940, probably by a drift mine. Subsequent investigations at the wreck site suggest she was blown in half. It must have been a grisly ordeal for the crew because it seems that some of them may have survived the blast and tried to escape from the remains of the vessel. The use of drift mines was something of an enigma since they were indiscriminate and just as dangerous to one's own ships as they were to the enemy's.

The crews never relished the experience of laying mines. There is an interesting description of this activity by U-34, a good example of a minelaying submarine in the Second World War. One of her tasks was to lay mines in the mouth of Falmouth Harbour, where there was 15m of water. Her commander, Rollman, had to give the crew a pep talk beforehand:

> U34 passed through the harbour entrance. To the left and right of her towered the mole heads, in a moment she was in the middle of the harbour itself, proceeding round a wide arc. 'Mines clear', then 'Mines clear for dropping' came the report from the torpedo room. 'Slow ahead both.' The whine of the dynamos rose a little. 'First mine away!' With a creaking and scraping the first mine fell clear. The whole ship's company froze to immobility, held its breath and listened. Would the Britishers hear the noise, and if they did, would they realize what it was? ... U34 proceeded through the enemy harbour in a broad sweep. The depth of the water was 13.8 metres which left her with a bare three feet of water under her keel.[8]

U-34 was laying magnetic mines, which would not operate until a certain time had elapsed, but it still took a great deal of courage and skill to lay such mines in the middle of an enemy harbour, making noises that were likely to draw the attention of the defenders. Incredibly they didn't. The submarine passed by a patrol boat on its way out and it was not detected. Even so, it was hard, risky work without the satisfaction of seeing a torpedo crash home. Only later, when reports were corroborated, could the submarine crew feel they had contributed to the war effort.

The depth charge was still the preferred weapon of the *Kriegsmarine* when it entered the war in 1939. In many respects the German versions were little different from those the British had developed. There were four types in service: WBD, WBF, WBG and WBH. The WBD had the biggest charge, 180kg of explosive, whereas the rest were supplied with a 60kg charge. The heaviest was the WBH with a weight of 240kg and a sinking speed of 4.35m per second. Their depth settings could be altered and the WBH could operate at 150m depth. Normally, six different depth settings were possible, in 15–25m steps up to a maximum setting. Blast radius was 8m for the WBD and 5.6m for the others. Rheinmettall, the great German arms manufacturer, was responsible for most designs of depth-charge thrower. Like the British, the Germans used both rail-mounted depth charges and single-barrelled throwers.

Italy, the other Axis power, was early into the arena of underwater weapons. We have already seen how Britain utilized Italian designs for some of its weapons and it is clear that several good mine designs were available for use in 1914. Elia had designed a perfectly reliable mine pistol, which the British adapted for their own purposes. Designs produced for the Italian navy were put forward by two Italian naval officers, Emanuale Elia and Geralomo Bollo. The

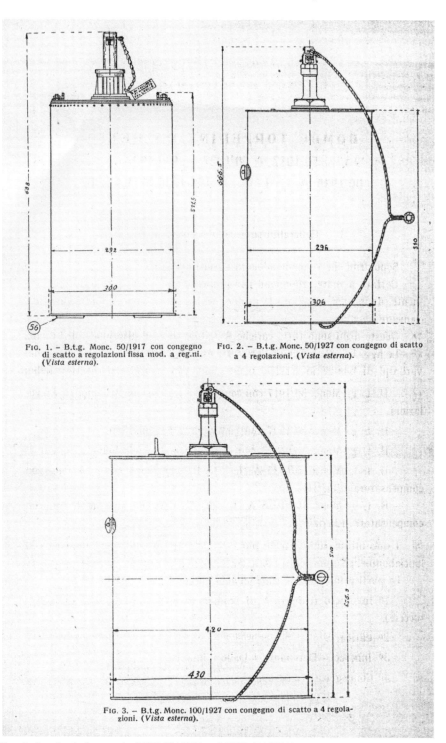

FIG. 1. – B.t.g. Monc. 50/1917 con congegno
di scatto a regolazioni fissa mod. a reg.ni.
(*Vista esterna*).

FIG. 2. – B.t.g. Monc. 50/1927 con congegno di scatto
a 4 regolazioni. (*Vista esterna*).

FIG. 3. – B.t.g. Monc. 100/1927 con congegno di scatto a 4 regolazioni. (*Vista esterna*).

Two Italian depth charges, the BTG 50/1936 and BTG 100/1936.

latter was a member of the Italian examining committee and his rivalry with another Italian officer, Scotti, had some effect on the Italian naval mining programme. In 1913 Scotti offered a mine design to the Italian Navy that was being manufactured by FIAT, but it was not taken up by the Italian

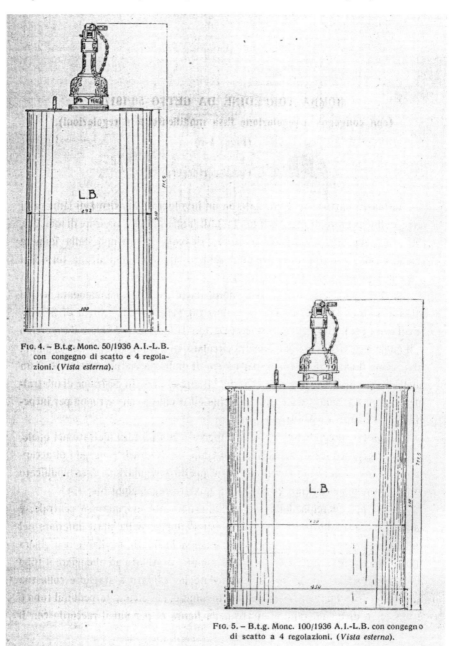

FIG. 4. – B.t.g. Monc. 50/1936 A.I.-L.B. con congegno di scatto e 4 regolazioni. (*Vista esterna*).

FIG. 5. – B.t.g. Monc. 100/1936 A.I.-L.B. con congegno di scatto a 4 regolazioni. (*Vista esterna*).

Two further Italian depth-charge designs, the BTG 50/1936 and the much larger BTG 100/1936.

Government, though a very similar mine – said to be a copy by Commander Bollo – was accepted.

Bollo's mine was made by the Tosi Company. It relied on projecting phosphor-bronze arms, which extended outwards from the mine body. These arms broke off when an enemy vessel made contact and water was then admitted into a chamber containing a hydrostatic valve. The water pushed the valve onto a detonator and the mine went off. Scotti did have some success with his counter-mining units, which were similar hydrostatically operated units to those manufactured by FIAT. These mines were dropped into the water and exploded at a certain water pressure or depth, thus setting off other mines. Whether this can be classed as a mine or a depth charge is open to discussion. Elia mines were heavily used in the Italian Navy, as were Novero and Gimnoti observation mines.

By the Second World War, Italy had decided to rely upon mines as a principal counter to the allied navy, even though their production capacity was not up to the job. The navy had a stockpile of about 25,000 mines spread around its naval bases. Most of the mines deployed were buoyant types operated by Hertz horn, with TNT as the main explosive filling. The *Regia Marina* experimented with many different types and in 1936 came up with the P200 mine. The Bollo mine was upgraded and the Elia mine, which had served the Italians well in the Great War, was also used in the Second World War.

As with the British, the Italians also used some imported mines, principally the Harlé mine and the Austrian C15. By 1939, Italian mines were mainly being produced by the Pignone Company of Florence. There had been a great deal of interplay between Italian firms and Vickers, many of whose mines were also made in Italy. Nevertheless, mines were always in short supply and that is why the Italians began to use German designs after 1941, when the Germans agreed to supply four types: the UMA, UMB, EMC and EMF. It is thought they supplied over 12,000 mines to the Italians, whose designs were good but in short supply. The P200 mine became Italy's mainstay and it was one area of weapons development in the Second World War where the Italians were successful in combating the Royal Navy.

By the Second World War many of the depth charges used by the *Regia Marina* were made by Pignone, but also by the Moncenisio and Scotti companies. The depth charge was known as the Bomba de Getto or BTG. A document in the Royal Naval Historical Branch details many of the different types of depth charges and their use. For example the A/130 could be used by ships, anti-submarine boats and aircraft. There is a description of the pistol; within the translation of the document, it goes as follows:

> This consists of a hydrostatic plate by means of which the hydrostatic pressure is gradually transmitted, as the charge

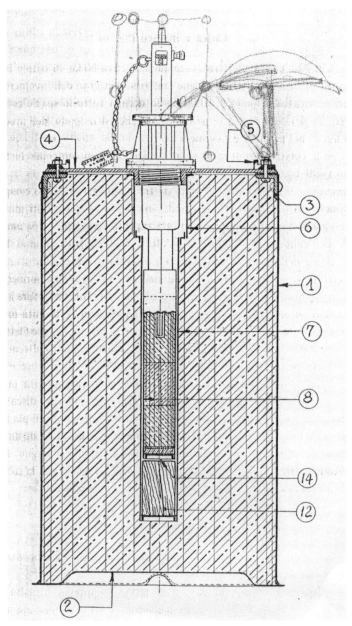

A rare cutaway drawing of the Moncenisio BTG 50/1917.

descends the spring underneath compressing it. According to the setting given to the device i.e. according to the distance of the connecting balls from the recess made in the slide, the striker is released at the required depth, due to the action of the counter spring on the hydrostatic plate, to hit the percussion cap causing detonation.[9]

This description is almost exactly the same as the hydrostatic pistol that the British first used, and the ball-and-groove device was subject to one of Herbert Taylor's claims against the United States. It may be that the Italians acquired the device during the First World War and copied it. If they didn't, it is a remarkable coincidence. As shown in the table, these Pignone depth charges came in three sizes.

Italian depth charges between the wars

Type	Charge	Weight	Length	External diameter
Moncenisio BTG 50/1927	50kg			
Moncenisio BTG 100/1927	100kg			
Moncenisio BTG 50/1936	50kg	64kg		
Scotti 43cm	100kg	128kg		
Pignone	50kg		700mm	280mm
Pignone	100kg		780mm	370mm
Pignone	150kg		830mm	420mm

The Scotti charge was supplied by a company set up by the naval officer mentioned above in the discussion of Italian mines. Italian depth charges relied on a hydrostatic pistol and operated at a maximum depth of 100m. One unique

Italian depth-charge throwers were quite sophisticated. This version is the 302mm 1934/1937.

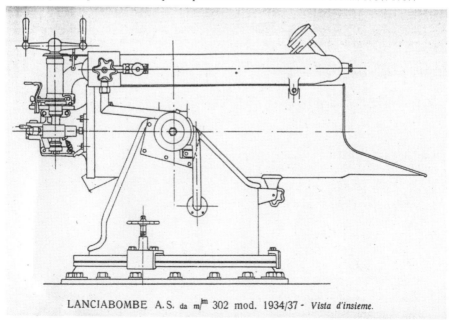

LANCIABOMBE A.S. da m/ᵐ 302 mod. 1934/37 - *Vista d'insieme.*

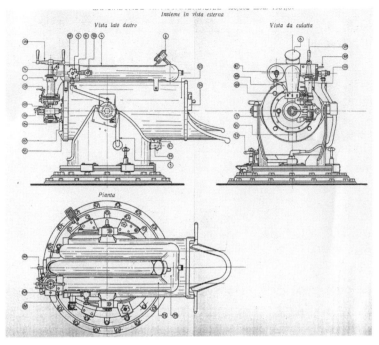

A technical drawing of the AS 432/302 Mod. 1934-37 thrower, showing the breech.

item used by the Italians was a flooding device, by which the depth charge could be rendered inoperable if it did not explode. This was an optional extra that could be purchased from the Pignone Company. The second table shows the depth charges that were in service by the middle of the war.

Italian depth charges used in the Second World War

Designation	Weight	External diameter
BTG 50/1917	62.5kg	600mm
BTG 50/1927	64kg	300mm
BTG 100/1927	128kg	430mm
BTG 50/1936	70kg	300mm
BTG 100/1936	130kg	430mm
BTG 150/1940	180kg	430mm
BTG 30/1941	42kg	300mm
BTG 60/1943	130kg	450mm
BTG 125/1943	180kg	450mm

The Italians were also able to produce a thrower that could take the complete depth charge and fire it from a tube; and the British produced an equivalent design, which never got beyond trials on HMS *Whitehall*. In fact the Italians produced two single-barrelled throwers, the Lanciabomba AS 432/302 Mod. 1934-37 and the Lanciabomba AS 302/1933 Mod. 1937. Both were short-barrelled, with a scooped baffle at the front, and the 432/302 was also able to fire the smaller types of depth charge with a tube inserted into the barrel. The ranges depended on the chamber pressure and typically the 432 could achieve a maximum range of 110m at 65 kg/sq. cm.

So what were other countries using? The Soviet Union was using a depth charge very similar to the Mark VII in British service. There were two types of charge, a 365lb version and a lightweight 70lb version, both mounted in welded steel cases.

Soviet depth charges

Type	365lb	70lb
Diameter	17in	10in
Charge	292lb TNT	55½lb TNT
Overall weight	365lb	70lb
Length	28in	16½in
Sinking rate	2.5m/sec	2.07m/sec

On both types of Soviet depth charge, the primer tube was screwed into the base of the pistol chamber and contained a lead oxide–lead styplate detonator, one tetryl primer pellet and three TNT primer pellets. The pistol is always the most important part of the weapon. The way this one worked was that water entered through a port and orifices in a diaphragm cup in the pistol. This in turn exerted pressure on a copper diaphragm. The pressure at a static depth of 10m was sufficient to force in a ball-release pin, until the retaining balls moved out of the groove and a spring-loaded firing pin moved down to fire the percussion cap.

This information comes from a technical manual published by HMS *Vernon* in 1956; it was intended to help naval staff identify and defuse foreign weapons. Again the system is almost identical to Herbert Taylor's design and the use of a ball-and-groove release mechanism seems to be almost universal for this type of device. It might be added that the staff at *Vernon* thought that the Russian charges were a little unreliable because they later stated that a variation in depth of about 3m must be expected when using these weapons.

The United States did not have a hydrostatically operated depth charge like the British D-type at the beginning of the First World War. The US Navy was at first armed with a float-and-lanyard type of weapon. The Mark 1 carried 50lb of explosive and could vary its depth from 25ft to 100ft. The Mark 2 depth charge was almost identical to the British D-type. Two more marks were introduced before the end of the war, the Mark 3 and Mark 4. The latter had a much larger charge, of 600lb. One American innovation was the Y gun, a double-throw depth–charge gun in Y configuration, where both arms were set at 45° of elevation. It could fire depth charges both to port and to starboard and therefore had to be placed at the stern of the ship. It would fire at up to 80yd range and thus was able to cover a wider area of sea.

Lieutenant Commander A J Stone designed the thrower and it was claimed to be an improvement on the British version. Even so, Thornycroft throwers and Y guns were fitted to US Navy ships and there seems to have been little difference between them. The Y gun could malfunction, since the propellent charges fired both barrels and sometimes a premature explosion could give a nasty shock to the crew. USS *Allen*, when chasing a submarine on 29 June 1918, found that one of her charges exploded at only 40ft under the ship, shaking it considerably.

By the time of the Second World War, the Mark 3 depth charge had been redesigned and an improved sinking speed of 8ft per second had been achieved. In the same way the heavy Mark 4 was redesigned to become the Mark 7, with additional weights to give it a faster sinking speed. With its case made from aluminium, the American Mark 8 was a step away from the original British design and had a magnetic pistol, which (as in the British versions) proved unreliable and was not produced in quantity. It was also equipped with a hydrostatic pistol should the magnetic one fail. All the previous weapons were of the standard oil-drum shape, but with the Mark 9 charge the US moved away from the traditional design.

The Mark 9 had a case like a teardrop, giving it an improved hydrodynamic shape. This type of charge entered service in 1943, carried 200lb of torpex and could operate down to 600ft. The United States had also developed an acoustic charge known as the Mark 14, which was trialled in 1944, but unfortunately it was still not fully developed by the end of the war. Somewhat unusually the Americans adapted the Hedgehog anti-submarine weapon, but not Squid. It was produced in 1942 in the United States and was considered to be a good weapon in the US Navy. The mounting was developed with electrical control and its use was probably more efficient on American ships because of this. Two projectors were devised, the Mark 11 and Mark 12, which gave an elliptical pattern or a circular one, depending on what was required.

France had a very sizeable modern navy at the beginning of the Second World War and had developed a range of depth charges that could be used by various vessels. They came with 200kg, 100kg and 35kg charges. Not surprisingly, perhaps, the British firm of Thornycroft had managed to sell some of its throwers to the French Navy, for use with the 100kg charge. The thrower was virtually identical to the Mark II thrower in British service, but with a 24cm bore. The home-grown M1928 mortar was trainable, which the Thornycroft weapon was not.

One of the great failures of the Imperial Japanese Navy was inadequate development of an anti-submarine programme. Their depth-charge system was heavily based on British designs and in the Second World War the Type 2 was the commonest in service. It had a filling of 102kg of explosive and the pistol allowed depth settings of between 30m and 145m. These depth charges were released by stern rail or by Y gun.

Chapter Seven
Interest from across the Pond

In 1917 Britain was at its lowest ebb in the war with regard to the sinking of ships by U-boats. Essentially, if Germany could sink ships faster than Britain could build replacements, she could place a stranglehold on supply by sea, forcing Britain to negotiate terms. As an island nation, the United Kingdom relied upon food imports to keep the population fed. In April 1917 the Germans were sinking 250,000 tons of shipping per week and these losses could not be sustained. The Royal Navy was not sinking enough U-boats and the industrial capabilities of Germany in April 1917 were such that, it was thought, she could build three U-boats a week. The mining of port exits and blockades of German shipping routes were not working, possibly due to ineffective British mines. Reinforcements were needed and Britain was hoping these would come from the United States.

There were about 120 U-boats available in February 1917 and this increased to 180 in November 1918, though no more than fifty were at sea at any one time. As the war dragged on, they became less and less effective. It is known that part of the reason for this was the adoption of the convoy system. Whilst there is much debate about who introduced the system, there were two distinct advantages to convoy. Firstly, it was a defensive measure that concentrated all merchant vessels at one point and quite often the convoy would pass undetected by the Germans and, secondly, if it was detected, it acted as a way of drawing in U-boats so they could be dealt with by the escorts.

On 6 April 1917, the United States entered the war on the side of the allies. The United States Navy was well aware of the U-boat threat, but it had no viable anti-submarine weapon. There was a good reason for this. The United States was initially considered by the allies as a neutral country and, to quote a history of US Navy ordnance, 'The construction of depth charges, and of their firing mechanisms, was guarded as most secret by the nations employing them'.[1]

The British Government received a request for assistance from Rear-Admiral William Sowden Sims, a graduate of Annapolis and naval attaché in Paris in 1898, who was a gunnery expert and commanded the Destroyer Force

Explosion of a mud mine at Horsea Island

The explosion of a mine on the mud at Horsea Island, near Portsmouth. George Malcolmson Collection

Atlantic Fleet between 1913 and 1915. He was captain of the battleship *Nevada* before being sent as a liaison officer to London in March 1917 and then assuming command of United States Naval Forces European Waters. This was followed by a number of specific requests by other US naval officers for equipment, including this one from William Dougald McDougall:

> American Embassy. Office of the Naval Attaché, London, 23 March 1917.
>   Dear Sir Graham,
>   I am writing to ask you if the Admiralty will kindly give me, for the use of the United States navy department, a full set of working drawings with explanations and instructions for the manufacture and use of depth charges for combating submarines.[2]

It has been suggested that the United States took the designs and adapted them to make them safer, but it is clear – from patent awards in the United States and examinations in Britain – that the American Mark II depth charge was the same as the D-type in use in Britain. Not only that, but a letter from Admiral Sims to Secretary of the Navy Daniels stated:

> We should send in addition to usual stores carried by our repair ships such stores in supply ships as our experience indicates will be necessary, such as boiler and condenser tubes, pipes and repair materials etc. As many depth charges as per drawing forwarded about 8 April should be made and forwarded as soon as practicable to relieve the present drain on British supply for their patrol craft and destroyers.[3]

This letter indicates that United States intended to copy the charge and supply the Royal Navy with the same charges. This request started a chain of events, which, for several British inventors, led to a long struggle to get recognition that their inventions had been used by the United States Government. Along the way several of the ideas, especially Taylor's and Gwynne's, were patented by members of the US Ordnance Department. The British Admiralty had accepted the depth-charge pistol and the primer safety device as standard equipment in the depth charge D-type, but was not able to produce enough for the war effort. When the United States entered the war, the manufacture of anti-submarine weapons was of high importance and too few were being produced by the critical year of 1917.

Jellicoe stated that the manufacturing capacity of Great Britain was often so seriously overstretched that many of the Admiralty's plans had to be delayed or altered in some way:

The Admiralty was, indeed, seriously embarrassed by difficulties in the adequate supply of mines and other means of destroying submarines as well as fast craft of various descriptions. The Admiralty, as was pointed out, was not doing what they wanted to do, but what they could do, both in the way of offensive and defensive action. The supplies of raw material and labour controlled in large measure the character and extent of the operations at sea.[4]

The need for the United States Navy to take over many of the anti-submarine and minelaying duties was critical and there is not the slightest doubt that it contributed greatly to the success of the anti-submarine war in the post-Jutland period.

The process by which these inventions were sent to the United States was started by the letter from the United States naval attaché to the Secretary of the Admiralty in March 1917. On 3 April, the naval attaché acknowledged receipt of five drawings. These were blueprints for the D, D* and G depth charges.[5] The Director of Torpedoes and Mines sent examples to the United States for their manufacture and Lieutenant Commander Mock of the Royal Navy took further drawings to the USA. Mock was then to begin work with Commander Fullinwider and Lieutenant Wilkinson of the United States Ordnance Bureau. According to Admiralty reports, the US Navy were considering a depth-charge design by Sperry that operated on the float-and-line principle and did not incorporate a safety device. The D-type was very different from this and therefore, according to at least one modern author, the Americans improved on the British version and then issued their own weapon. This clearly was not the case, as was later shown by the American registered patents for the pistol and primer safety device, which were exactly the same as the British ones – as the US Patent Office agreed when Taylor and Gwynne challenged the patents.

The Admiralty stated, when handing over the drawings at the start, that any use of these designs should not prejudice the originators of the designs from lodging patents in the United States. Despite these protestations of integrity, Lieutenant Commander Fullinwider (Patent 1372617 for the primer safety gear) and Lieutenant Minckler (Patent for the depth-charge pistol) patented the designs in the United States, a bone of contention not resolved until the 1930s. Admiral Sims himself wrote back to the Admiralty on 24 April 1917:

> I can assure you that the handing over of these drawings will not be regarded by my government as publications pending lodgement of patents nor will they otherwise prejudice any patent rights.[6]

The US Bureau of Ordnance was being disingenuous when it said:

> The bureau considered that the design submitted to it as being the latest British type was unsafe according to American ideas, and also

unreliable, and completed a development of its own. Not until this, its own design, was ready to test did it learn that the mechanism submitted to it, as being the British, had proven unsatisfactory.[7]

From this, a new depth charge was supposed to have been designed, the Mark II, and this project was led by Simon P Fullinwider. If this was an improvement in the design – and this author has his doubts – and if the British design was considered unsafe, why then did the US Navy order a further 15,000 D-type depth charges from Britain in 1917?

The invention of military devices and the encouragement of their inventors formed a well-established concept in the Admiralty in the First World War. In fact technical staff were employed in order to establish what these inventions were and who should be recognized for them. In 1923 Arthur Edwards was just such an employee and he was known as a Technical Assistant to the Admiralty. In his own words, his job was:

> the consideration of inventions put forward, and, where secret patents are taken out, drafting specifications and seeing to the lodging and amendments and so forth; also comparing the similarity of inventions to decide who in the service is the first true inventor.[8]

By having such an officer, the Admiralty was recognizing the need to deal with the problem of patents and designs that were almost invariably reliant on the creativity of an individual.

Naval officers were encouraged to develop ideas and experiment with equipment, but – by Article 415 of the King's Regulations – all their inventions became the property of the Lords Commissioners of the Admiralty. Taking control of intellectual copyright may be thought severe, but it ensured that in time of war the Admiralty could introduce new ideas without delay or risk of a lawsuit. The Admiralty did pay gratuities to the inventors, though they didn't have to, and a great deal of grovelling and scraping was required to get an idea looked at.

As we have seen, Burney had the ear of the Admiralty and it was clear that he was able to get access to Jellicoe relatively easily, but for Taylor it was another matter. Burney did not ask for payment for his ideas, though he did suggest to their lordships that it might be easier if he was allowed to take out patents in allied countries or sell them drawings of his inventions. The Admiralty would get a royalty and some of this would be paid to Burney. It seems here that Burney was well versed in ways of manipulating the Admiralty to get a patent. He came away with the rights to sell in other countries, rights which he profited from in the end.

Taylor had to find his patronage in other ways. It says a great deal of Captain H L Skipworth at HMS *Vernon* that he supported Taylor in his claims. This may have been because he knew that Taylor was a prolific inventor and somebody to be cultivated. Several of the later inventions that came from HMS *Vernon* carry Skipworth's, Sturgeon's and Taylor's names on them. But, and it is an important point, many inventors had no support from their superior officers. To this author it is clear that Skipworth supported most of Taylor's claims because he believed that he was entitled to them. From what we know of Taylor's personality, which is only what we can glean from his letters, he may have been a difficult man to deal with on a day-to-day basis. Perhaps he did not have the sophisticated bargaining skills that Burney had; at any rate, Taylor received from the Admiralty only a single *ex gratia* payment in full and final settlement of his claims. Luckily for Taylor, he was able to negotiate a deal with Vickers, which paid him handsomely.

Although patent law is very complex, especially where the invention of military equipment is concerned, it is clear that the ideas of Taylor, Gwynne and Sturgeon were patented by others in the United States, even though they were given to the United States Government as part of a war emergency programme. This also raises the question of the inventors' financial reward. It is a common perception that, in the world wars, individual needs had to be sacrificed to the imperative of collective survival, but the individuals' gain from these inventions was potentially considerable. Taylor and Gwynne also had British patents and they petitioned the Admiralty for some reward for their inventions. In the end, Taylor received £5,000 from the Admiralty for his work. In comparison with his private patents with Vickers, this was a piffling sum, but even so £5,000 in 1920 was worth a great deal more than it is today.

The statement from Taylor's attorney was straight to the point and the inventors were clearly aggrieved that US naval personnel had immediately patented their ideas, given in good faith to the United States Government:

> These inventors, therefore, hold basic patents in Great Britain and United States for the Primer Safety Gear and the Depth-charge Pistol, as well as in every other important maritime nation. It will be seen that the United States Government, itself, endeavoured to secure patents for these devices through the medium of Officers and employees of the United States Navy and that the United States Patent Office in each instance has recognized the prior invention by, and the rights of Alban L Gwynne and Herbert J Taylor.[9]

In Britain, Admiral Philip Dumas was Head of the Department of Torpedoes and Mines at the time of the invention of the pistol and safety gear. He stated that:

> I was so satisfied that such a device would be of great value, in safeguarding against premature explosions, that I advised the Admiralty that Primer Safety Gear should be fitted generally to all Mines and similar explosive weapons.[10]

The Admiralty was already aware of the need for a depth-operated explosive charge – and had tested some without much success – but Dumas advised the Admiralty that they should include Taylor in their plans and get HMS *Vernon* to proceed with the ideas with his assistance.

One question may already have arisen in the reader's mind: was it the American officers who were at fault for using known designs or was it the US Government that expected them to gain the best technology then available for their navy? The question may never be answered but the inventors' attorney in the case, A R Johnson Jr, seems to imply that it was actually the US Government.

Simon P Fullinwider was a key figure in the arena of naval mining and explosive ordnance. The modern author Hartmann describes him as a commander in the United States Navy, who retired in 1914 but was recalled in 1917 to head Desk N at the United States Navy Bureau of Ordnance.[11] He was involved in the development of United States Mark VI antenna mines. Even at the age of seventy, Fullinwider was recalled in 1940 to become involved in the underwater weapons programme the USA was then developing. There is no doubt that he was central to the work of the Bureau of Naval Ordnance.

Fullinwider had registered a patent for the Primer Safety Gear in the United States on 26 January 1918, patent number 1372617. When Gwynne challenged this in the United States in July 1921, Fullinwider was represented by Paul A Blair, Head of the US Navy Patent Section. The fact that he did suggests that 'this was considered to be a matter of some importance to the United States'.[12] What happened was that Blair stated that Gwynne's design was negligent and that there was a lack of diligence with regard to the design. This did not wash with the United States examiner, who told the Naval Ordnance people that they had no right to raise such issues as this and accordingly awarded priority of the invention to Alban L Gwynne.

When Herbert Taylor eventually got the Admiralty to agree to file an application in the United States for a patent for his pistol he found that there was already a claim to this design by a Mr C T Minckler, under patent number 1368569. Perhaps unsurprisingly, Minckler was an engineer of mines and explosives in the Bureau of Ordnance of the United States Navy. The brief in support of the petition to the Commission for the Adjustment of British Claims states:

> Although Engineer Minckler, an employee of the United States Navy, held a prior United States patent for the Taylor Depth-charge Pistol, an investigation conducted by the United States Patent Office resulted in the issuance of the United States Patent 1514743 to Mr. Herbert J Taylor for the Depth-charge Pistol. The record discloses that the prior patent applied for by Minckler was predicated upon the plans and specifications of the Taylor Depth-charge Pistol provided by the British Government, and concerning which patent protection was promised.[13]

Minckler made very little attempt to challenge the fact that his design had come directly from the drawings supplied from the Admiralty and, to be fair, as soon as this was pointed out, he dropped his claim – a claim against the British Government for using what he said was his design. The United States Patent Office came out of this squabble with flying colours. They appear to have carried out meticulous investigations into the origin of the designs and brought the case to a rational and just conclusion.

There was now no objection to both men's claims that the United States Navy was using their inventions, but whether they would be paid for their inventions was a much more thorny issue. It was calculated that the United States had used 54,996 depth-charge pistols and 49,996 sets of primer safety gear up to the time that the commission met. On the basis of previous patent cases, the claimants expected payment at a royalty of £4 per depth charge, divided equally at £2 for the pistol and £2 for the primer safety gear. These figures implied a payment of £109,992 for the pistols and £99,992 for the primer safety gear, a king's ransom in the 1930s. In fact the attorneys and the claimants both knew this was probably too much to ask for and as result of some deliberation they actually asked for $37,498 for the pistol and $34,998 for the primer safety gear.

At the hearings it had been mentioned that Vickers-Armstrong, the British armaments giant, had decided to take up Taylor's and Gwynne's patents in order to produce their weapon for export outside the United States and Great Britain and were willing to pay considerable sums to do so. They had agreed to a contract of £60,000 for both devices. This clearly would not be paid all at once, but it would make both men very comfortable for the rest of their lives. Without it, Taylor would have had to make do with an Engineer Grade One's salary at HMS *Vernon*. If the US Government agreed to pay even the reduced sums, the two men would never have to worry about finance again. Whether Taylor actually received payment from the United States Government remains unresolved.

There remains one final comment to make about the question of patents and their financial benefits. One of the final letters in the small amount of correspondence among the Taylor MSS, donated to the Museum of Naval Firepower in Gosport, is to Herbert Taylor's wife from Vickers-Armstrong in 1967. In reply to Mrs Taylor's request for a further payment on her late husband's patent rights, the letter says:

> Depth Charge (Submarine Mines) Royalties.
>   With further reference to the above subject and our letter of the 5th instant, we have now heard from our South Marston and Weymouth works to the effect that no sums are held as due to your late husband in connection with the above. As previously advised, production of the item referred to has long since been discontinued,

VICKERS LIMITED
ENGINEERING GROUP

TELEPHONE
BARROW-IN-FURNESS 3366
TELEGRAMS
VICKERSENG BARROW-IN-FURNESS
CABLEGRAMS
VICKERSENG BARROW-IN-FURNESS
TELEX BARROW 6597

VICKERS - ARMSTRONGS
BARROW ENGINEERING WORKS
BARROW-IN-FURNESS

YOUR REF

OUR REF E/ACC/JD

23rd January 1967

Mrs. R.F. Taylor,
'Tawany',
1a, Kings Road,
Emsworth,
Hampshire.

Dear Mrs. Taylor,

Depth Charge (Submarine Mines)Royalties

With further reference to the above subject and our letter of the 5th instant, we have now heard from our South Marston & Weymouth Works to the effect that no sums are held as due to your late husband in connection with the above.

As previously advised, production of the item referred to has long since been discontinued, and the possibility of any further Royalties becoming due in such respect is very remote.

Yours faithfully,
FOR VICKERS LIMITED,

Chief Accountant,
V-A Barrow Engineering Works.

The letter to Taylor's wife from Vickers in 1967.

and the possibility of any further royalties becoming due in such respect is very remote.[14]

It may be that the Taylors had spent all the royalties received from Vickers, but the amount that could have been gained from the US Government would have been considerable. It seems unlikely that Mrs Taylor was the beneficiary of any monies coming from the United States.

Chapter Eight

Between the wars

There is no perfect mine yet …. Some years ago the phrase Periodic Finality was coined. This may be defined as the stage in which various tentative designs are crystallized into the current standard design which is produced in bulk for the service.[1]

The years after the First World War were difficult ones for naval design. The government had said that Britain would fight no new wars for at least ten years and the corresponding budget cuts forced many projects to lie dormant. The Board of Invention and Research was dissolved in January 1918, after which the main person responsible for research was the Director of Experiments and Research, who co-ordinated the various research groups. On the Admiralty Board, the Third Sea Lord was in charge of naval research overall, but for our purposes the Director of Torpedoes and Mines was head of all things explosive. In 1920 the Chief Inspector of Naval Ordnance (CINO) was given the task of inspecting torpedoes and mines, including depth charges and explosive paravanes, answering to the Director of Torpedoes and Mines.

The Pierse Committee in 1920 made some important statements on the development of naval technology: firstly, that the weapons requirements of the navy had to be defined by the user – in other words a naval officer; and secondly that scientific research had to be left to civilian scientists and designers who had the necessary training. This was summed up in paragraph 53 of the committee's report:

That inasmuch as the active service seagoing naval officers cannot remain sufficiently long in the administrative posts connected with ordnance to acquire an adequate knowledge of the scientific problems which arise in the course of the research, designing work and manufacturing processes which result in the finished article, and as the civilian scientist has not the seagoing training which is necessary to ensure that his efforts are being applied in the right direction, it is essential that there should be associated with the users and the scientists a body of naval officers with sufficient sea training to be able to appreciate the sea requirements and the problems arising in connection with the use of naval ordnance, and also possessed of the necessary scientific training to fit them to guide the work of the scientists.[2]

This statement explains the approach taken by the Admiralty with regard to the development of naval weapons. In the light of experience in the First World War, it was a logical and sensible step to take.

The submarine had proved its worth in the First World War but most post-war discussions were still about the surface fleet. Many of the naval *cognoscenti* had become alive to the fact that the submarine was now firmly entrenched in the naval arsenal. The Washington Naval Treaty dominated much of the discussions in the 1920s, but Britain was not expecting to go to war against an alliance of Germany, Japan and Italy, as she eventually did. Most discussions revolved around the size of various fleets in navies around the world. The feeling in the air was one of disarmament, but as a wise old man once said 'everybody wants peace, but we all want peace with advantage'.

At the end of the discussions in the 1920s, limits had been imposed on certain fleets, while others got away with a sleight-of-hand reduction in their naval forces. The emphasis was on the capital ship and those who were unable to match the might of the major navies began to look for something to redress the balance. In the case of Japan it was the air force and the torpedo, whereas Germany looked to the pocket-battleship and the submarine. This imbalance in naval power shaped the forms of warfare that dominated the coming conflict.

Britain's naval policy between the wars relied on a strong anti-submarine element, but in the period 1919–39 this was pushed aside to give priority to the RAF obsession with long-range bombers. In naval staff circles, the idea still held that the convoy was a defensive strategy. This was why, when convoys began again in 1939, anti-submarine vessels were concentrated in hunting groups. Soon it became clear that the convoy would draw U-boats to it, so they could then be attacked.

Detection took a great leap forward in the form of echo ranging. The idea was to tune to the frequency of an incoming echo, which would indicate the depth and distance of an enemy submarine. The ASDIC – an abbreviation referring to the Anti-Submarine Division – became the British answer to the problem of underwater location.[3] At the end of the First World War, the idea was being considered. The French appear to have experimented in 1915 and 1916, and kept the British Board of Inventions and Research informed, but it was the scientist R W Boyle who carried them much further forward in Britain. In March 1918, after much experimentation, Boyle proved that a submarine could be detected from 500yd away. The Admiralty ordered twenty early ASDIC sets in June 1918 and the sonar was born.

ASDIC was an active system, rather than a passive one. It relied on generating acoustic waves that travelled through water and could bounce off the hull of a submarine. If they were reflected, they could be detected. However, post-war cuts in defence spending meant that, for some years after 1918, further development was slow. However, by the beginning of the Second World War, both Germany and Britain had developed reliable inboard sonar sets for the detection of enemy vessels. The problem was that the system did not automatically trigger the attack and so there was always a delay between detection and firing.

Back in Portsmouth, in 1919 those who remained at HMS *Vernon* moved ashore to Gunwharf. At the end of the war, many of the civilians who had been taken on for war work were being paid off because of budget cuts. In the experimental department that Taylor had set up, it was very difficult to keep a team together. But he was resilient and eventually managed to get the whole workshop transferred to the civilian sector. He was re-graded in 1919, becoming an Engineer Grade I. Taylor's design career for the Admiralty started in August 1921, when he relinquished control of the workshop and took up duties as the designer of mine accessories and depth charges. There were two engineers assigned to these duties, Taylor on Grade I and an assistant on Grade II. Further changes occurred in 1928, when these two engineers were placed under the control of the Senior Technical Officer.

In 1922–3, HMS *Vernon* was reorganized again and the Mining School became part of HMS *Vernon* (M). An important development was the establishment at Portland in 1924 of HMS *Osprey*, which became the anti-submarine branch. This left a somewhat curious relationship between *Vernon* and *Osprey*. As E N Poland put it,

> Its creation also meant that the Mining Department at Vernon was left with the responsibility for the provision of anti-submarine weapons and training of personnel without being involved in the development, use and maintenance of detection equipment, or the evolution of Anti submarine strategy and tactics.[4]

This was to have far-reaching consequences in the Second World War when *Osprey* began dabbling in weapons development, producing the Fairlie mortar, as we shall see later.

One of the first problems of the post-war period was improvement of the main service mine, the HII mine. Experiments were carried out with different kinds of mooring and a different shape. The improvements were such that mines could be laid at a depth of 6,000ft, instead of 3,600ft. The new designs were eventually embodied in the Mark XIV mine. The main themes of the inter-war period were improvement of the buoyant mine and the development of controlled minefields. The processes of fabrication and production were also addressed. In 1935 the British started to develop another kind of antenna mine, which eventually became known as the Mark XX.

Moored mines were useful in defence, but Britain really needed something that would work in an offensive way. There were drawbacks with moored mines: they could be easily swept with the right equipment; it was possible to avoid them, even in the middle of a minefield, because they were generally thinly laid for safety reasons; and they were affected by the tidal action of the sea. The best improvement was to produce a non-contact mine, set off by magnetic or acoustic influence. The M Mark I was the first of its type. It was clear from the First World War that dip-needle mines were not reliable. What was required was a mine that would operate reliably when a ship passed by and in this year the CR (coiled rod) method of detection was born. This consisted of a long rod of mu-metal that had a small electrical current induced in it when a vessel passed over it. Nevertheless, a moored magnetic mine had only a slightly greater sphere of influence than a contact mine. The challenge was to design a mine that was not moored and could be laid without a sinker.

Taylor was involved in the development of the CR rod as used in the magnetic mine. He certainly laid claim to it in his deposition to the Admiralty, when he talked of the CR F-type mine. The idea of the CR mine can be seen as parallel to the proximity fuze of 1943, which exploded near the target aircraft. In this case the vessel had only to be close to the mine. Experiments in 1933 had shown that a mine could be detonated if a vessel passed within 5ft. All this research and development resulted in the M Mark I mine, the first true British magnetic non-contact mine, which came into service in 1939. It is important to remember that this mine was still a moored mine, but its area of operation was much greater than that of a contact mine.

Between the two wars, Taylor made an important contribution to the success of the magnetic mine. Among other things he developed the sensitive relay, from a laboratory prototype, and designed the anti-countermining switch. These, together with the CR rod, were extensively employed in the British magnetic-influence mine circuits used in the 1939–45 war. Many of Taylor's designs from this era are as significant, if not as critical, as the invention of the depth-charge pistol, but being placed as an assistant to an officer effectively demoted Taylor. Furthermore, in 1932 his section came under a Principal Technical Officer and in 1936 he was placed under the Chief Technical Adviser dealing with special designs. He seems to have resented his position and clearly felt he had been passed over. This may have been reflected in his desire to gain financial benefit from his work, since he had gained little status. Even so, he worked throughout the Second World War and many of the projects bear his stamp of originality.

On 25 May 1939 the Superintendent of Mine Design at HMS *Vernon* submitted an application for an award for Mr H J Taylor as he had, in his eyes,

HMS Tarpon, *a destroyer used for minelaying duties and depth-charge trials at the beginning of the Second World War.* Herbert Taylor papers

'shown unique inventive genius not only in the designs mentioned in his application but in general experimental work of the Department'.[5] The document also mentions some of the details by which Taylor had improved the production of certain parts but also considerably reduced the cost. He had devised a new form of mine shell construction. He suggested spun-over mouthpieces for the watertight joints. This improved the body of the mine considerably, by increasing its strength and reducing its weight. It became standard in all mines of the following marks: Mark XIV, Mark XV, Mark XVI, Mark XVII, M Mark I and L Mark II.

About 15,000 mines using this construction were ordered and some Mark XVII mines are still around today. Even without this construction, keeping mines from leaking was a constant problem. As an engineer in the Second World War stated,

> A continual headache was leakage into the mineshell from a faulty bung or cover (or a faulty inserted bung). I seem to remember a litany of complaints about how awkward they were to seat reliably. To be fair, setting clocks etc. and refitting bungs on the afterdeck of a minelayer going flat out in bad weather was no joke.[6]

The saving for the Admiralty from Taylor's improvements was £10 per mine. This added up to a saving of £150,000, a very considerable sum in those days.

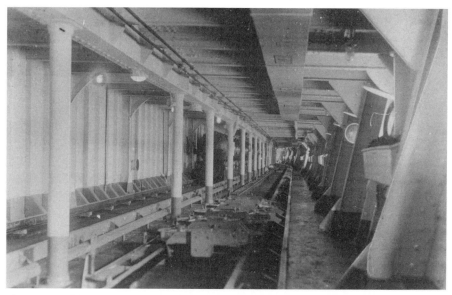

A rare view of the minelaying rails on board an unknown vessel during the First World War. George Malcolmson Collection

The Admiralty did give Taylor an award, as the Superintendent of Mine Design had asked, but not until 6 September 1943. They paid him £5,000 for his work, with the words:

> Their Lordships desire that Mr Taylor's attention be called to the vital importance during the present National Emergency that all citizens should save to the utmost of their ability and lend their savings to the Government for the prosecution of the war. Accordingly, Mr Taylor is asked to state whether he is prepared to receive the whole or part of the award in the form of National Savings certificates, Defence Bonds or other National Securities.
>
> Their Lordships desire to call attention to the difficulties that arise in considering a claim in the form submitted by Mr Taylor embracing inventions and designs made over a period of some twenty years, some items of which could well have been the subject of separate claims made at a reasonable time after the date of proved adoption.[7]

This slightly miffed rejoinder is interesting, being made in 1943, four years after Taylor had been asked to re-enter the Ministry of Defence to assist in naval matters. It does appear there was some resentment at being asked to pay Taylor anything at all. It is not fully clear from the source whether this was his one and only claim, but it appears that it was. If so, one wonders that such an ungrateful organization should have benefited by the efforts of Taylor and others at all.

Explosion from a depth charge at the rear of HMS Tarpon. Herbert Taylor papers

In the 1930s, research was still being carried out on the depth charge and the pistol. The pistols were assembled and tested at the Royal Naval Armaments Depot at Priddy's Hard, Gosport. This site on Portsmouth Harbour had become one of the navy's most important logistical, storage and repair sites, from the late eighteenth century onwards. By the 1930s it was a large semi-industrial complex with its own piers and workshops. Perhaps more importantly, the Inspectorate of Naval Ordnance was based there and the site stored or repaired depth-charge parts and explosive paravanes. The Mark IV** pistol was tested between March and May 1930. Also in 1930 the trawlers *Redwing* and *Vernon* were used to test pistols from here, to see if they were still usable. The pistols were dropped on a line and tested by water pressure to see if they still fired. All were set to a depth of 50ft and fired after about 5.25 seconds. Although the majority of the pistols fired, it was found that some did not and Priddy's Hard was blamed for the poor assembly of some items.

The depth-charge thrower too was undergoing some design changes. Quick-firing breeches were developed for the throwers in 1919 and two designs were considered, one known as the Malta design and the other from Thornycroft. The term 'quick-firing' in this case really meant 'quick-loading', derived from the fact that the propellant was enclosed in a brass case. The first quick-firing gun had been introduced in the Royal Navy in the 1880s and the Hotchkiss 3-pounder and 6-pounder guns were the first large-bore quick-fire guns put into service. They were a response to the introduction in the 1870s of Whitehead's torpedoes and the small fast vessels that carried them. The threat led to increasing armament on warships, to try to stop the torpedo boats launching their weapons.

Nordenfelt and Hotchkiss had introduced machine guns of 1in and 37mm calibres, which used a fixed round – that is, a brass cartridge containing the propellant and attached to the projectile, which could be loaded in one go. The torpedo boats got bigger and began to protect themselves by putting their boilers behind their coal stores, and a so a larger, quick-firing round was needed. This eventually became the Hotchkiss 3 and 6-pounder guns. The type of cartridge used for these guns was widely used as a propellent charge, not only for the gun, but also in a cut-down version for the depth-charge thrower. These cartridges began to be widely used for torpedo propulsion, engine starting and even, after the Second World War, in aircraft ejector seats. The venerable Hotchkiss gun went out of service only in the 1990s, when its last role as a saluting gun was given up. The original breech of the Mark II thrower was screwed into the firing chamber, so a mechanism was needed that was easily opened in one swift movement, enabling a brass case to be quickly inserted into the chamber.

Returning to the new breech firing trials, it became obvious that the breech designed in Malta was overcomplicated and susceptible to premature firing. The test officer trying out the hand-operated system in June 1919 said that, if the safety pin was left out, the thrower could be set off by bearing down too hard on the firing lever. It was therefore decided to drop this version after comparing it with the new breech produced by Thornycroft. The British firm had improved their breech by adding various safety devices, such as an explosion chamber that had to be separated from the barrel to be loaded and a spring-worked indicator that showed the operator when the breech was properly locked. Their design was accepted with some modifications after this trial.

Present at this trial and there for his valuable opinion was Mr R A Sturgeon of the Mining School. Sturgeon was also involved in a programme of testing for a new lightweight arbor (sometimes called a carrier) in 1919. The old version, as described previously, weighed 150lb and this weight was thought prohibitive on smaller ships, especially if several arbors were needed. It should be remembered that one of these arbors was used every time a depth charge was laid. The carrier was at first designed in a similar way to the naval stick bomb at the end of the 1914–18 war and consisted of a standard metal tray fixed to a wooden shaft. Three wooden discs were attached to the shaft, one at the base and two more equidistant along the shaft. The idea was that the discs would act as an obturating pad and at the base was a sealing diaphragm. Enough impetus could be imparted to the base of the carrier to throw it the required distance, in this case 40yd. Trials at Gunwharf in 1919 with a Mark II thrower indicated that the shaft broke on firing and the tray could be damaged in the process.

Many other types of lightweight carriers were designed and tested to overcome the problem. In 1922 a Lieutenant Commander Barret was testing a different design of lightweight carrier to determine its effectiveness. In this case the carrier seems to have been made so that the stalk was the same diameter as the interior bore of the barrel, but its interior was hollow. This meant that the explosive gas was forced inside the carrier stalk, pushing it out of the barrel. This alteration increased the muzzle velocity considerably and therefore the range. These tests also revealed that the Mark IV pistol might fire on striking the water, depending on the initial setback – in other words, the shock of firing. The light carrier improved the range of the thrower from 51yd to 76yd.

Herbert Taylor commented on this test that it seemed there was a limit to the distance that a Mark IV pistol could be fired; certainly with the light carrier the pistols appeared to explode prematurely on hitting the water. This was thought to be because the trajectory of charge and carrier was higher and they also descended on a steeper trajectory. Taylor thought that the introduction of the C-type pistol would overcome this. He recommended that the hollow stalk be made at Woolwich.

Versions of the light and heavy throwers tested in 1922

Light carrier

Weight of charge and carrier	524lb	572lb
Weight of carrier	921lb	91lb
Average range	77yd	75yd
No. of rounds fired	7	7

Standard carrier

Weight of charge and carrier	576lb	642lb
Weight of carrier	162lb	162lb
Average range	52yd	50yd
No. of rounds fired	6	6

This table, taken from the Depth charge trial book, records the tests by Barret in 1922. A certain number of cases occurred in service where a depth charge fired from the thrower exploded on impact with the water, resulting in serious accidents to the personnel of the attacking vessel. This was amply proved by the accident aboard HMS *Barranca* in 1917.[8]

In the First World War, the types of launcher used were many and varied. It was only at the end of the war that a hydraulically operated system was in place; otherwise, depth charges were launched, depending upon the ship, either by rail or by thrower. It was not just ships that were used to operate the thrower; an interesting remnant exists in the Royal Navy Submarine Museum, which may sound somewhat odd. Because the K class submarines were always considered fast enough to accompany the fleet in operations, some of them were fitted with a depth-charge thrower. These steam-powered submarines were a disaster and several were lost in accidents. It has never been clearly explained how the depth-charge thrower was meant to be used, but it must be the only example of a submarine mounting.

The next important development in the inter-war period was the production of a ground mine. In 1935 the mine department at HMS *Vernon* knew about the dangers of the magnetic (or acoustic-influence) mine to its handlers. The staff requirement for such a mine was laid down in 1936: the mine needed a special shape, because aircraft might lay it, and this limited its size. Magnetic firing systems were developed or improved in Britain and Germany. More significantly, the Germans explored the possibilities of laying them from aircraft and by the beginning of the war they had a viable weapon.

The CR (coiled rod) unit devised for the magnetic mine could easily be adapted for a ground mine and in some ways was even more suited to the shape of the ground mine. British ground mines were long and thin, to suit aircraft, so a long CR rod down the axis of the mine body was an ideal solution. By September 1939 sufficient laying trials by aircraft and ranging trials against ships had been carried out to ensure that the mine was ready for service. Interestingly, the success of these trials for aircraft-laid mines led to a requirement for these mines to be used from surface ships.

Although he had reached retiring age in 1936, the outbreak of the war in 1939 found Taylor still working for the Admiralty. Taylor was an old man with health problems, but he worked on with his usual enthusiasm and success to produce designs for river mines, beach mines, sabotage and beach-clearance weapons, X-craft charge cases and other items that played an important part in operations. Taylor thus made an outstanding contribution to British victories in two world wars and to the success of the mine design department. The United States Navy adopted the depth-charge pistol and used 54,996 of them under the patent of Herbert J Taylor. The name of Taylor continued the association with depth charges and mines, because Taylor's son Jack had begun to work at Leigh Park House and carried on what his father had started.

Chapter Nine
Prima donnas, crackpots and misfits

At the beginning of the Second World War, the combatants had different strengths in anti-submarine weaponry: for example, the Germans had perfected the airborne magnetic mine and the British had developed the ASDIC set, which gave a whole new dimension to the search for submarines. It seems Germany was not ready to prosecute an underwater war and only when the war began was it decided to use the submarine to disrupt Britain's sea lanes. Both sides had relatively small numbers of vessels dedicated to the war under water: the Germans had fifty-seven U-boats and the British had sixty submarines, with nine being built. The German navy also had twenty-two modern destroyers and was building eight more, whereas the Royal Navy had about 145 destroyers, as well as 20 trawlers with anti-submarine equipment and various patrol craft. However, most British warships were far from British waters, dotted around the empire.

The fall of France heralded a new U-boat offensive, since French bases gave them easy access to the Atlantic. The years 1940 and 1941 were difficult ones for British shipping, when U-boats could slip undetected in the vast open areas of the Atlantic Ocean. The convoy system had been implemented immediately, but the Germans began to use concentrated U-boat attacks, known as wolf packs, to attack convoys. In 1940, U-boats were attacking British and allied vessels constantly and the strain this put on British resources was considerable.

At HMS *Vernon* (M), efforts were concentrated on two areas: increasing the production of depth charges, pistols and their ancillary equipment and (to fulfil an Admiralty requirement) increasing the numbers of anti-submarine vessels. The depth charge remained the principal anti-submarine weapon. It has been calculated that, at the end of 1940, there had never been more than ten U-boats at sea at any one time, so finding them was rather like trying to find a needle in a haystack. Nevertheless at least thirty-three had been destroyed in the first six months of the war, in which time 4,000 depth-charge attacks had been carried out. Yet it was the Germans who were on the offensive and had demonstrated the will to carry out an unconventional and devastating naval war, and not just with U-boats.

The magnetic mine incident

As mentioned earlier, the main ways of exploding an underwater mine in the First World War were by contact or observation. A lucky discovery in 1940 showed that was no longer so. It was to have far-reaching consequences and, not surprisingly, the Mine Design Department was involved. Germany now had a magnetic mine that was easy to deploy, of a type unknown to the British. Early in 1940 British ships were being sunk in alarmingly large numbers off the east coast of Britain and the Admiralty had begun to wonder how the Germans were able to lay their mines without being detected. A team from HMS *Vernon* was mobilized to try to find out.

Lieutenant Commander J G D Ouvry was the man with the most experience of non-contact mines. He had had experience of minelaying on the cruiser *Inconstant* during the First World War. His contemporaries described him as a taciturn thinker and he was ideal as one of the officers detailed to deal with the new threat. Another member of the team in this incident was the civilian scientist A B Wood, who had had a very long career working for the navy, first with the Board of Invention and Research in the First World War and then working on hydrophones with Captain Ryan at Hawkcraig. The Mining School at *Vernon* had been the basis of hydrophone research as well as weapons development and Wood was transferred there in 1922. After the Great War he remained with the scientific service at Parkeston Quay, near Harwich, and by the time of the Second World War he was working with the Mine Design Department. Wood was appointed Superintendent Scientist at the Admiralty Research Laboratory at Teddington, Middlesex, and the development of magnetic and acoustic mines, with their counter-measures, became part of his remit.

The truth of the tale was that the Germans had perfected an aircraft-laid magnetic mine. By a freak accident, some of the new mines were found off the coast at Shoeburyness in Essex. The German High Command, specifically Admiral Raeder, had decided to test the device by dropping a number of them in the Thames, using Heinkel He59 aircraft. The British suspected this and kept a close watch on the shoreline for this kind of sortie; eventually a couple of eagle-eyed Lewis gunners managed to attack one of the Heinkels in the act of laying mines. The aircraft dumped their load on the shore at Shoeburyness and fled.

This team from *Vernon*, including several petty officers, had the task of discovering just how the German magnetic mines worked. Winston Churchill took a personal interest in the work and the whole process was one of those salient moments when British and German scientific minds were pitted against each other. The team went to have a look at one of the weapons and at some personal risk examined it for clues to its operation. As Ouvry and other naval personnel rendered the weapon safe, it is known that part of the mine was removed for examination to Woolwich Arsenal by a team of scientists from the Mine Design Department – and one of those was Herbert Taylor. Wood was also called to have a look at the mine and its mechanism.

A magnetic mine lying on the bottom of the sea could detect a ship passing over it. Such a mine did not float, so buoyancy was not an issue. A sinker was not required, so its weight was less. These mines carried only explosive and firing mechanism; being smaller and lighter, they were perfect for laying from aircraft. However, as Dr A B Wood later pointed out,

> It is clear that the German mines of pivoted magnetic type operated on changes of vertical magnetic field – in the direction of N-pole downwards – a feature common to all ships in N latitudes. Assuming all German mines possess this characteristic (although it certainly does not apply to British M mines) then a simple method of making ships immune at once presents itself, i.e. to magnetise the ships so as to have no north-pole downwards.[9]

This theory led to British ships being de-magnetized or de-gaussed, as it was known, and hence saving lives.

New quarters

In 1939, the Mine Design Department was still at HMS *Vernon* at Portsmouth, but the massive increase in staff – both civilian and naval – meant the department had to move to an office block on Commercial Road in Portsmouth. These offices were particularly vulnerable to air attack and the *Luftwaffe* were determined to bomb Portsmouth out of existence. Certain sections of the Mine Design Department were therefore moved away from the town to Leigh Park House, about 2 miles from Havant. This house no longer stands but it was, until 1959, part of what is now Staunton Park. The Leigh Park estate is best known for the work of Sir George Staunton, who had purchased it in 1820 and lived there until his death in 1859. The dispersal of staff was planned, because the branch of the Mining Department known as *Vernon* (M) was sited at nearby West Leigh House and the naval staff of HMS *Vernon* responsible for the trials section of the Mine Design Department travelled widely to stations around the United Kingdom. Part of the unit was placed in West Leigh Cottage.

By 1941 administrative facilities had been established at West Leigh Cottage, new trials areas had been set up on Loch Long in Dumbartonshire – at the head of the loch, at Arrochar, and at its mouth at Baron's Point, where mines were tested – and in 1942 a ground mines facility was established at Weston-super-Mare. The need to experiment, manufacture and test weapons led to all sorts of outstations being set up. At Weston, by 1943 the base at Birnbeck Pier on the north side of the town was used for all mine-dropping tests by the Aircraft

Torpedo Development Unit. This facility was later moved to the airfield at RAF Locking, about 3 miles south of Weston. Parts were manufactured at Fareham, close to Gosport, and German mines were examined at a disused quarry on Butser Hill, near Buriton, 15 miles north of Portsmouth.

The examination of German weapons and the process of trying to predict their operation brought a whole new dimension of work to *Vernon* and its associated units. A reorganization meant that officers were in charge of a British and allied mine section and a German mines section. A further officer was required for all trial work. The enemy mining section was responsible for the recovery and disarming of German mines and practising these procedures. In addition they were to:

- create instructions for carrying out disarmament;
- create confidential handbooks on disarming foreign weapons;
- instruct others in the disarming of mines;
- take charge of examination and stripping of German mines at Butser Hill, Buriton;
- deal with all mines washed up within Portsmouth Command.

This was a great deal of work for such a small staff and quite often the lines between the two departments were blurred.

Much of the work at West Leigh House was in section T2, which has great relevance to the story of the depth charge and the mine. Allan Pilledge, who had spent some of his youth in Singapore, came to Portsmouth in mid-1939 with his father, a dockyard worker. In 1942 he entered West Leigh House as an Assistant Experimental Officer and joined T2, the section that tested mining and depth-charge equipment and components. The section was housed in the old stables. It had a small office close by and an old workshop, which was used to create models and test rigs so that tailor-made engineering items could be manufactured. The connection with HMS *Vernon* was such that a small office was kept there for people from West Leigh House, when they were on sea trials or using the mining tank. Mr Pilledge described this as follows:

> This tank was a cylinder about thirty feet in diameter and some sixty feet deep, filled with water, which had a platform suspended on wire ropes which could be raised or lowered to any depth. It had originally been built to check the operation of mine sinkers during the development of buoyant mine designs but proved really invaluable for a multitude of jobs including, I think some of the early underwater swimmer suits.[10]

The Head of T2 section was Arthur Mitchell who, like many of the staff, was employed on a temporary basis, for the period of the war only. Mitchell had been a schoolteacher in his pre-war days. One of the more famous inhabitants was the Chief Scientist, P M Blackett, who won a Nobel prize for his work on nuclear fission. In 1943, the future Sir Robert Boyd joined the Admiralty Mining Establishment at West Leigh House, where he was given strong encouragement by scientific colleagues such as Harry Massey, David Bates, Tom Gaskell, John Gunn and Francis Crick. There were three depth-charge experts in this section: Jack Taylor, Jimmy Simms and Sydney Robinson. The design office had a J M Kirkby, based up at Leigh Park House. It can be seen that there were many intellectual as well as practical scientists at West Leigh or Leigh Park House.

One of the people included in this reorganization was Jack Taylor, a chip off the old block who naturally ended up working for the Admiralty. Both Herbert Taylor and his son had been involved in a motor engineering business between the wars. As a former member of staff at West Leigh House, told the author: 'I recall he was sharply aware that his father had not been rewarded after the first war as perhaps he should.' Jack Taylor took over the role of depth-charge pistol expert that Herbert had carried for so long. In Mr Pilledge's view, 'Like his father, I think he was full of ingenious ideas and had a good engineering brain'.[11]

It seems that Jack Taylor became less and less involved in depth-charge work as time went on, and more and more involved with demolition work, some perhaps inadvertent:

> I can certainly verify that at the end of the war Jack was doing work on cutting things open with shaped charges using the then new plastic explosive. This was very much up Jack's street, though he got himself into quite a pickle when he tried to burn out the explosive in a partly opened charge case, which ended in a low-grade detonation that sprayed the Weston-super-Mare neighbourhood with gobbets of flaming TNT.[12]

Herbert Taylor, now an old man, was still working on designs at Leigh Park House and spent at least some of his time working on demolition and X-craft side charges.

According to Edward Wadlow, a former worker at Leigh Park House:

> The largest room served as a conference room and doubled as dining room for the senior staff. Rooms on the first floor were allocated to the Superintendent, Captain Riley, and to his assistants, Commander (later Captain) Lane and Commander Nicholls. Various members of the civilian staff were housed on the first and second floors, with the drawing offices mainly on the ground floor. The purchasing staff, and those responsible for instruction manuals, were on the first floor, while the canteen was located near the one-time kitchen, with the telephone exchange upstairs in one of the rooms at the upper rear of the house.[13]

Many of the staff who were working on projects frequently had to travel, between England and Scotland for example. One such project was the northern mine barrage, which extended along an underwater ledge to Iceland and continued across the Denmark Strait to Greenland. This necessitated an extended mining effort at Kyle of Lochalsh, initially under Admiral Wake Walker, a very stern commanding officer, but later under Admiral Robert Burnett.

HMS *Vernon* (M), as it became known, was a place of unusual characters; of necessity it was important that creative, able people were drafted into the department. At the time, Alan Pilledge was a junior rating serving at Leigh Park House. He described the place as full of 'crackpots, prima donnas, and misfits'. It seems that this was a standard way of engaging able people – to allow them their head as it were. HMS *Vernon* had future Nobel Prize winners and a whole host of unusual characters who would not have fitted into a purely military background.

Their work was very varied and often included the manufacture of components as well as sea trials. Most of these were carried out at Spithead and they could be lively affairs:

> We did sea trials at Spithead, not that far from Ryde Pier, using an elderly steamer, based in HMS *Vernon*, which was capable of laying out a long trot and of laying mines and retrieving them. Typically we tested the capabilities of new or altered designs and components to withstand the concussion of the explosion of the next mine in the row [often known as countermining]. On occasion a trial required a buoyant mine to be laid and left for a while. On recovery, the sinker was opened with some caution for it was a favourite hiding place of conger eels, and a big eel in a bad temper needed watching.[14]

The scale of work at the Mining Department continued to expand. The needs of new projects and the demand for training could only be met by the use of skilled civilians and reserve officers in a training as well as working role. Minesweeping training was moved to HMS *Lochinvar* on the Firth of Forth, but because the departments had been so dispersed a special section at the Admiralty was created and led by Captain J S Cowie. His book *Mines and Minesweepers* is full of insights into the arcane world of the mine. As part of this reorganization, a team of scientists was brought to Leigh Park House to work on acoustic and magnetic mines. Of Taylor's role there in this period, Poland says:

> Among those responsible in this enlarged area was H J Taylor, who had been involved in the development of the depth charge in the First World War. He was still designing underwater firing mechanisms which could not be countermined, and concentrated on relays and explosive devices to be used in beach clearance.[15]

Improvements in depth charges

Although the Royal Navy had made great progress with the design of depth charges, these devices still had their limitations at the beginning of the Second World War:

> [A] pattern of five Mk. 7 depth charges [was] being dropped in the form of a centred square. The leak-hole depth pistols fitted to these charges were provided with six settings from 50 feet to 500 feet depth. The asdic gave no direct measurement of the depth of the U-boat and the depth to be set on the pistols was decided largely by guesswork; this was not as inaccurate as it might at first appear since it was claimed that some indication of the depth was given by the range of loss of contact by the main asdic beam.[16]

Experience in the First World War, working with stern-release depth charges, had shown that the percentage kill rate of a ship armed with depth charges was quite low when using the standard five-charge pattern. The Mark VII depth charge, more inertia-proof but little different to the D-type, was still in use and it was decided that a ten-charge pattern would be far more effective – so, for every Mark VII used, a heavy Mark VII was added. The heavy Mark VII had a far faster sinking rate, which was critical to the success of the attack because it could increase the depth at which an attack was made. The heavy Mark VII had a weight added, which meant that the axis of the charge was vertical and it sank at a rate of $16\frac{1}{2}$ft per second.

This practice came into use in 1940 and the number of charges could be increased to fourteen if required. Obviously, more charges were used in each attack and at least half of them would sink to a greater depth. A U-boat might travel at 3 to 6 knots under water and this was just not fast enough to avoid these large charges; and going deeper might not avoid them either. The heavier version of the Mark VII required new types of launchers to deploy it. This was because specific patterns had to be delivered to capitalize on the advantage of the heavy charge. When ten charges were fired, five light charges were fired in a centred square formation, with five heavy charges making intermediate sides in a diamond pattern on top of them. The heavy charges were fired from throwers inclined at 45° along the ship's side. When a fourteen-charge pattern was used, five heavy charges, then four heavy and finally five normal charges were launched in turn.

In 1942 it was agreed to replace amatol by minol as an explosive filling for the depth charge. Minol increased the blast range – typically, a submarine with a pressure hull of steel $\frac{3}{4}$in thick would be affected at a distance of about 26ft – and the effect within the blast radius was also greater, increasing the chances of doing damage. It was calculated that the use of minol would increase the chances of forcing a submarine to the surface by 50 per cent. A far greater improvement in the effectiveness of the depth charge would have been the use of magnetic influence. The Mark IX charge was developed for just such a purpose, but was never given the high priority it should have been and the weapon never entered service.

Depth-charge pistols too were being improved. It was obvious at the beginning of the war that U-boats were capable of diving to about 300ft and the standard depth-charge pistol could be set down to this depth. After 1943

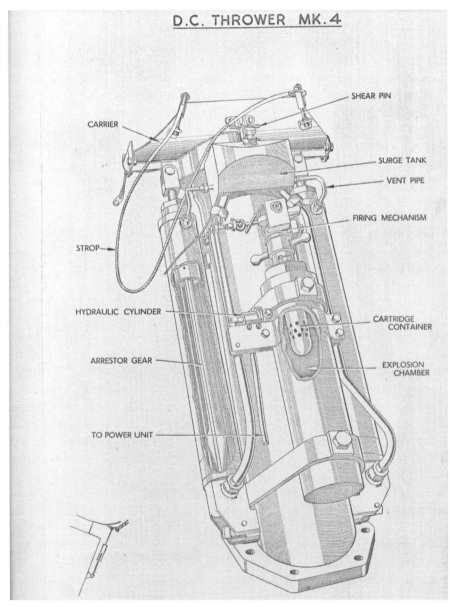

A contemporary cutaway drawing of the Mark IV depth-charge thrower.

U-boats were built to dive much deeper and so a pistol was required that would operate at far greater depth than had been envisaged. The Mark X pistol was an improvement on the previous marks since it gave a pre-selected firing depth, with safety features particularly suited for use in aircraft, mainly in Coastal Command. By the spring of 1941 an aircraft-launched depth charge was introduced that could fit in the RAF 250lb bomb rack; it was known as the Mark VIII. The Mark XIII pistol soon replaced the Mark X and was almost immediately superseded by the Mark XIV, which was specifically designed for use with aircraft.

One of the more difficult problems encountered in the Battle of the Atlantic was the fact that ten charge patterns were difficult to mount and handle on deck, especially in a rough sea. It is not uncommon to see images of escorts at the time with depth charges and arbors all over the deck. In the early designs of thrower, the arbor was lost once fired. To reduce the number of arbors carried and improve efficiency, a new thrower was introduced, the Mark IV. This thrower had a captive arbor mounted in the barrel, restrained by two pistons fitted with arrestor rods either side of the tray. When fired, the tray abruptly shot forward and was held at the length of its travel, firing the depth charge into the air but retaining the arbor. The charge was normally fixed to the carrier/arbor by a wire hawser. This in turn was held taut by a tumbler hook. When the thrower was fired, the tumbler hook gave way against the body of the charge, releasing it and retaining the hawser.

Finally came the introduction of the Mark V thrower, which continued the lightweight concept previously described. The thrower needed to be smaller and lighter than the Mark IV, but keeping the arrestor rods and carrier retaining features. The breech was to be designed by the Chief Engineer of the Armaments Department (CEAD) so it could be fired electrically or mechanically by hand (but not by hydraulics). As usual Thornycroft were given the project and they went away to see what could be done. The breech was to use a 3-pounder cartridge, but it did not have to conform to the loading arrangements used on previous weapons. When it came, it was a significant improvement. The firing gear could be cocked and fired several times, but the significant design feature was that the firing spring was not cocked except when firing. The breech opened by a slide-sideways-and-then-lift action and it was quick to operate. This meant that several charges could potentially be launched quickly.

By January 1944 the thrower was nearly ready for trials. It was decided to fit the new design to HMS *Highlander*, a destroyer then fitting out at Troon, Ayrshire. When trials started, they were carried out by HMS *Vernon* (M) and it was found that electrical firing was not as reliable as had been hoped and mechanical firing was not tried at all. As with the other models of thrower, the optimal range was about 75yd away from the ship. The thrower was taken back to Thornycroft to be modified, but when it was returned it was found that the weapon did not stand up to the rough handling that the trials had imposed on it, and further changes were needed. In May 1944 the *Highlander* set off for more sea trials, to test the thrower further. Even more modifications were required before it was eventually accepted into service and even then the Mark V was earmarked to replace Mark II throwers only. This meant that ships fitted with Mark IVs would probably retain them to the end of the war.

In 1942, to meet the demand for design engineers and trials officers, it was decided to post more staff to *Vernon* (M). Two officers were appointed to run the long-range depth-charge thrower and the aircraft depth-charge projects; two were to deal with demolition; one was to rewrite the depth-charge handbook; and one was to act as trials officer. At this time one of the largest depth charges yet made was being tested. The Mark X depth charge contained a ton of explosive and could be used from the stern of Captain Class frigates. The official history tells us:

> In December, consequent on the allocation of a large number of old destroyers to A/S escort duties and which would not, therefore, require torpedoes, it was decided to develop a large '1-ton' Depth Charge as an additional A/S weapon to be fired from the torpedo tubes.[17]

The Mark X was trialled in March 1942. Although the 1-ton charge was successful, very few were ever used, but those that were used recorded a kill rate of 50 per cent. As with the Mark VII, a heavy version of the Mark X depth charge was developed, which sank at a faster rate.

In 1943 there was a great improvement in the efficiency of standard depth charges. The fourteen-charge pattern was done away with, because it tended to damage the pistols. The exploding charges all going off in close proximity had a counter-mining effect. Refinement of drills and new indicator gear allowed the charges to be handled much more reliably and effectively. The Mark VII* charges were being filled with Minol II explosive.

The success of aircraft combating U-boats during 1943 was reflected in a change in tactics by the Germans. They could either fight it out with the aircraft, increase their evasive diving depth or avoid detection. This last tactic resulted in the *Schnorkel*, a device that allowed U-boats to charge their batteries while travelling under the surface. In response the Royal Navy developed a new depth-charge pistol, the Mark IX***. This could operate at depths between 700ft and 850ft. Lothar Günther Buchheim describes his experience of such a depth-charge attack:

> We are defenceless: at this depth we cannot make use of our weapons. The first crashing sledgehammer blow causes everyone to shudder. One man who wasn't holding onto anything staggers and almost falls. The second blow makes all the lights go out. White

cones from flashlights cast circles into the darkness. Someone calls for new fuses. Another explosion as massive and precise as its predecessors. What about the buoyancy cells?[18]

This grinding attack could go on for hours and it obviously affected the men's stress levels. Busch, in *U-boats at War*, said that,

> when you're being depth charged, everyone looks to the officers. I had one officer – he was off duty watch at the time – who actually went to sleep during depth charging! He didn't wake up until some fittings came adrift and landed on his head, then all he did was give a sort of peevish grunt, mutter something about 'restless times' and immediately doze off again.[19]

This apparently casual approach belied the fact that most men were terrified. Busch stated that the same officer had adopted a sort of stoical view on death. When asked about the right direction to travel in a minefield, he stated 'Doesn't matter, really. If you wake up tomorrow, you'll know you were right, that's all'.[20] In a U-boat, the key man during a depth-charge attack was the hydrophone operator. He was the link to the officer and acted as the eyes and ears of the ship. Interestingly the operator would not call out directions of the attacking ship, but give it in a communications number. Verbal communication had to be quite guarded so as not to panic the men.

Depth-charge attacks could be very intense and prolonged. During a raid on Convoy RA.66, U-427 unsuccessfully attacked two of its escorts, the Canadian destroyers HMCS *Haida* and *Iroquois*. The escorts fought back and dropped a total of 678 depth charges on U-427's believed position during a hunt lasting several hours. Luck and, no doubt, skill enabled the U-boat to escape on the night of 29 April 1945, but such a relentless attack was not unique. It was not unusual for submarines to endure attacks of up to 30 hours.

Depth charges were not used only for anti-submarine work, but also for anti-convoy purposes. The charge was attached to an oil drum and delivered by a coastal defence craft. The idea was that the drum and charge could be dropped together and the depth charge would hang by a pendant underneath the drum at a depth of 30ft to 60ft. The deeper depth setting could be set on the charge and so a delay was incorporated. It would be dropped in the way of convoys and thus the charge effectively became a drift mine that would cause quite a bit of damage when it went off. According to the technical history this device was introduced in July 1943.

In his book on the battle for Crete, Anthony Beevor hints at the use of depth charges for a more invidious purpose. As part of the invasion follow-up, after the parachute landing by the Germans, a mountain infantry unit was embarked on a number of caiques that were to sail to the island. They were intercepted by the Royal Navy and subjected to a bombardment, which destroyed the boats and left most of the mountain troops in the water. It has been alleged that at least some of those men were killed by the shock waves created by dropping depth charges in the water. This method of attack is very rarely referred to, but it is possible. The battle for Crete was a vicious combat and it is not unlikely that unorthodox methods were employed.[21]

The Royal Ordnance factories became the centres for preparing depth charges for the Royal Navy and their number increased from three to forty-four between 1937 and 1944. Production was divided between engineering factories, making metal components such as casings; explosive factories, which made materials like TNT and cordite; and finally the filling factories, which produced finished weapons. There were factories all around the country, for example, Risley, near Warrington in Lancashire, and Swynnerton in Staffordshire.

Aircraft-laid mines and depth charges

As early as 1940, the A series of mines began to come into service. In British terms they were truly revolutionary. Marks 1–4 were independent non-contact mines, at first magnetic but later capable of being detonated by acoustic influence. These weapons became the principal offensive mines of the Second World War and were made in large numbers. The first mark was designed to drop from 18-inch torpedo dropping gear, because there was no suitable long-range aircraft available. According to E N Poland, the first sortie was by Handley-Page Hampdens of No. 5 Group, which laid mines in the estuaries off German ports. Alterations to the Fairey Swordfish led to the use of 'Stringbags' as minelayers in the early part of the war. In fact they even laid them off the coast of Oran so that the French fleet, then under the control of the Vichy government, would not be able to escape if negotiations failed.

One critical mining activity during the Second World War was the laying of mines in German ports and sea lanes. This was much more easily done by aircraft. Ground mines that could be laid from the air would be deadly to the Germans and would certainly be an advantage for the side that could develop them. It came down to the Mine Design Department to do much of the development work. The early German lead in this kind of weapon came as an unpleasant surprise to the British. Laying mines and depth charges from aircraft requires a different design from the ship-laid mine. The size of the weapon itself is limited by the size of the aircraft, the load it can carry and the size of the bomb bay.

Ground mines lent themselves well to being laid by aircraft. The terminal velocity of the aircraft-laid mine was of great importance, because the mine contained many sensitive electrical devices that would be damaged on impact with the water. This was normally done by adding a parachute to the mine to slow its descent and the parachute housing was placed at the end of the mine case. In British service the designed terminal velocity was about 200ft to 250ft per second, which required a relatively small parachute; the Germans preferred a bigger chute but it gave a similar rate of descent of 75m per second. British mines had a fairing, which gave good air handling but was intentionally knocked off the mine once it hit the water. If one looks at an aerial-laid ground mine of the Second World War, one can see that the end opposite the parachute is chamfered at about 20°. This was to prevent the mine following its aerial trajectory on entering the water; otherwise it would reach the sea-bed very quickly at shallow depths. The shape of the nose further reduced the speed of descent once the mine was in the water.

The sweeping of ground mines required a completely different process than that of buoyant mines. They were generally detonated by remote action. Complex firing circuits were devised to make counter-mining difficult and these required magnetic or acoustic impulses at certain frequencies and time intervals to make them explode the mine. This meant there was also a constant battle between the designers and the enemy to devise ways of avoiding activating the mine.

The 1943 campaign certainly proved that a U-boat on the surface was a vulnerable vessel. In that year, Allied aircraft sank 139 U-boats. Aircraft could search large areas of sea and some of the longer-range planes could carry depth charges, machine guns and mines, and so represented a potent weapon. The main aerial depth charge dropped by British aircraft was designed by the Admiralty Mining Department. The RAF's first attempts to drop depth charges were made at Gosport with the old Mark VII depth charge, but this proved too large for an aircraft to handle and a limit of 250lb was set for aircraft-laid depth charges.

Because the Lockheed Hudson aircraft of Coastal Command had a small bomb bay, the depth charge it carried had to be 11in diameter and 38in long. A Mark VIII depth-charge primer was developed for use with this Mark VIII version. By 1940 this depth charge could be laid from a height of 200ft, but its entry into the water was problematic since the shock of impact could affect the pistol. Aircraft became one of the decisive factors in the battle against the U-boat in the Atlantic. Once aircraft were equipped with reliable depth charges and machine guns, and could use radar to detect the submarine, the U-boats were doomed.

Later depth charges were developed for different capabilities. In the middle of 1941, aerial depth charges such as the Mark VIII were only any use in deep water. It was clear that the best time for an attack was when the submarine was on the surface and a shallow-firing depth charge could be most potent against such a vessel. Three requirements were decided upon for aerial depth charges: increased striking velocity when hitting the water, shallow firing and greater reliability, to try to eliminate the possibility of a premature explosion. To answer the first need, a new pistol was tried, the Mark XII. This had no safety features and only one setting. It was meant to counteract the enormous back-pressure when the charge hit the water, but was in fact a failure.

The Mark XVI pistol became standard for shallow-depth explosions in surface attacks: it was made viable for an explosion about 22ft down, by using a weaker spring, removing the safety rod and spring-loading the orifice plate. The problem of shallow firing was overcome. A weaker spring in the pistol did not improve the firing parameters, so it was decided with the Mark XIII pistol to increase the number of water-entry ports to make the pistol operate more quickly. The Mark XIII was finished in April 1942. The shallow-firing depth charge also needed some form of retardation when it hit the water, to prevent it from diving deep. The solution was to add a concave nosepiece and a tail section fixed with rivets made of aluminium. The tail broke off and put the charge into the right attitude to slow its descent. This new depth charge was known as the Mark XI and was very successful indeed.

Instead of adapting naval pistols, it was eventually decided to develop an aircraft depth-charge pistol. The resultant Mark XIV was designed so that it had a large internal volume, to hold more water, so it did not require a weak firing spring and it had only one shallow-firing setting. This device did not have a safety primer device, but used a process known as back-flooding to make it safe. The Mark XI depth charge, with Mark XIV or XVI pistol, was accepted into service in September 1942. Once the aerial depth charge was combined with Coastal Command aircraft and crews, a very potent weapon emerged. Indeed, various modified versions of the Mark XI depth charge were still being used by the Royal Navy in the 1990s.

As an example of the kind of attack possible, we can look at U-927, commanded by *Kapitanleutnant* Jurgen Ebert. She left Norway in January 1945, heading for the English Channel on her first operation. On 24 February a Leigh-light-equipped Vickers Warwick of 179 Squadron, flown by Flight Lieutenant A G Brownsill, sighted her. The Leigh light was a 20 million-candlepower lamp in a retractable pod below the aircraft, for searching at night. The aircraft ran in on the U-boat at a height of 75ft and dropped six depth charges. The submarine was never seen again, but was considered to have been sunk by the aircraft.

A second example is U-681, which was attacked by a Consolidated Liberator aircraft on 10 March 1945, again on her first patrol. She was already damaged when the Liberator of 103 Squadron of the US Navy began coming in from astern. A second attack followed and the U-boat was sunk, with only eleven survivors. There are many attacks recorded by aircraft on submarines, but once there was good liaison between aircrews and their naval counterparts the aircraft could drop flares and markers, and shadow the submarine. This made the U-boat's job twice as hard and accounts for the high proportion of losses in 1945.

Once the Mark XI charge was perfected, a new requirement was issued, to develop an air-launched depth charge that could be dropped from a much higher altitude. The idea was put forward in August 1943. The requirement was for a 250lb depth charge that could be dropped from 1,500ft, but could detonate in 15ft to 20ft of water. This was technically difficult, but it was necessary because U-boats carried anti-aircraft guns and some were being armed entirely as Flak vessels, with the aim of attacking aircraft only. One difficulty was that the charge would behave differently in air and in water: good flight characteristics did not guarantee good underwater characteristics. The first type was designated the Mark XIV and this had an angled nose to orientate the charge on water entry. It was tested at an airspeed of 120–200 knots and worked very well. Unfortunately, when testing was complete, it did not enter service because a new requirement had been issued for a two-depth aerial depth charge. This design was intended to counteract the *Schnorkel*. The resulting design eventually became the Mark XV depth charge, but it was not used in combat because the war ended before it could be put into production.

Life for people at the naval test establishments was not always as safe as those fighting on the front line might have thought. Test staff were not without the threat of death or destruction. On one tragic occasion, one of the staff of HMS *Vernon* (M) and the whole aircrew with him were victims of a mistaken attack. Coastal Command reported an aerial attack on a submarine in which the aircraft and the submarine had disappeared. It turned out that a test was in progress on the Scottish west coast involving an aircraft dropping a string of depth charges. The first batch was dropped, but they exploded on the surface of the sea and set off the second batch, still on the aircraft, destroying the aircraft and killing the crew together with Charles Bound of the Mine Design Department.

These premature explosions resulted from the way the stiffening hoops were welded to the casing of the depth charges. (Incidentally, the interior of the casing was covered by shellac varnish, made from insects!) On pre-war cases, the hoops had been seam-welded, but in wartime production this was altered to tack-welding, which left cavities between the hoop and casing. When the casing hit the water, the shock waves generated in the air-space between hoop and casing were enough to set off the amatol, which was more volatile than previous fillings. This made them sensitive to concussion. A similar sort of problem in 1950 caused the explosion at Bedenham Pier, in which several thousand tons of explosive went sky-high, smashing windows as far away as Winchester.

Chapter Ten
Ahead-throwing weapons

In 1942, U-boats were attacking targets just off the east coast of the United States, where no coastal convoys had been organized and where illumination restrictions were not applied. The Germans took full advantage of this opportunity to sink nearly 500,000 tons of shipping between January and September 1942. The month of June was particularly dismal and the result would have been catastrophic if the Americans had been unable to build vessels at the prodigious rate they did. U-boat losses, on the other hand, were beginning to rise. All of this culminated in a bitter battle between the end of 1942 and June 1943. In that month, all U-boats were withdrawn from the Atlantic because their losses were unsustainable. When they briefly returned, losses were again high. In the first half of 1944, for example, forty U-boats were lost to depth-charge and Hedgehog attacks.

Why were so many U-boats being sunk in 1943–4?

Hedgehog projectile stowage.

Were surface ships now more effective because of new weapons? Were improved underwater weapons now destroying more submarines? Aircraft have been mentioned as hunters of U-boats, and radar and other innovations made aircraft even more effective, so were they what made the difference? All these improvements – in aircraft, underwater and surface weapons – would give allied forces the command of sea and air.

Squid and Hedgehog
Once the depth charge had been proved as an underwater weapon, practical problems began to show themselves. It was clear that depth charges had to be dropped in salvoes or patterns. On surface ships, they were usually dropped from the stern and this meant the vessel had to pass over the U-boat on the run

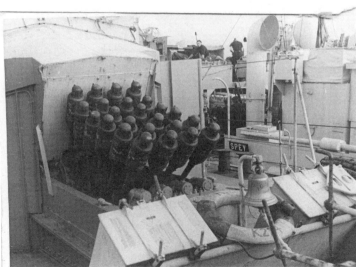

A fully loaded Hedgehog system, with projectiles trained in the upper photograph.

in to lay its depth charges. The ASDIC oscillator in the bows of the vessel lost contact with the enemy when it was still about 200yd ahead. Therefore there was a blind spot just before making the attack. To obviate this, the navy required a weapon that could be fired ahead of the ship, out to where ASDIC contact was not lost. This may all seem somewhat academic, but it was critical to accuracy because submarines could make very fast directional changes, allowing them to evade attack.

The long-range depth-charge thrower
The development of ahead-throwing weapons was not a co-ordinated affair at the beginning. Discussions began in 1940 to design a trainable depth-charge thrower that could be mounted in the forecastle of ship. After various discussions and tests, the idea of a trainable thrower was abandoned in favour of the forward-firing, long-range depth-charge thrower. In 1941 HMS *Vernon* and Thornycroft Ltd discussed the possibility of making one. Thornycroft were talked into producing the weapon, which consisted of a bronze alloy base and a tube of rolled boiler plating. The breech element had a thrower cartridge and expansion chamber. The angle of elevation of the weapon was 50° and when it was tested it could throw a depth charge about 330yd, using a cordite charge of 16oz.

Thornycroft constructed five such throwers for trials aboard HMS *Whitehall* in July 1941. The ship had her number one gun removed and the five throwers were fitted to the forecastle. The throwers were operated electrically. It took eight men nine minutes to reload the chargers and special loading davits were fitted to the ship. After trials on *Whitehall*, four throwers were fitted to HMS *Diana* for further testing in 1942. The experiments were relatively successful, but it was decided that Hedgehog, another ahead-throwing system being developed at the same time, would be a more effective anti-submarine weapon.

The idea had not been killed off in January 1942 when trials were carried out at Weston foreshore in Southampton to see how depth charges would behave when fitted with aircraft tails. The depth charges now measured 4ft 6in, making them larger and more difficult to handle. Three rounds were fired at a maximum range of 362yd and it was found that the charges were very poor aerodynamically. Some damage was endured by the charge. In April 1942 further trials were carried out – in concert with Captain Barret of the Department of Torpedoes and Mines, Commander Rogers of the Mine section of HMS *Vernon* and Commander Hutchinson of the Naval Ordnance Inspection unit at Priddy's Hard – and these were much more satisfactory. Six rounds were fired at the same distances as in the January trials and all were found to be relatively sound. There were two types of thrower, Thornycroft's design being fired tail-first and that from HMS *Vernon* being fired nose-first.

This led to further discussions and by August 1942 the Department of Torpedoes and Mines at the Admiralty had decided that it wanted more from the long-range thrower. The new requirements were that it should sink faster

HMS Whitehall, *showing the long-range depth-charge throwers installed on the foc'sle.*

and be fired on a wider arc, and that the explosions should not damage the ASDIC sets. In order to do this the impulse charge and the length of the thrower barrel both had to be increased, and the thrower need to be mounted lower on the ship. Simple cordite charges in brass cases were used in the chamber, mounted parallel to the main barrel. The system used a pistol to detonate the charge and the resulting gas was led from a chamber on the barrel side into the bottom of the barrel to push the depth charge out.

Hedgehog projectiles in flight.

In the end, despite extensive trials and some success, it was decided that the long-range depth-charge thrower was not viable. It is easy to see why: extensive changes were needed to make the depth charge stable in flight, the pistols were still not reliable when fired from the thrower, and the recoil of the throwers could damage the deck of the ship, so that extensive reinforcement was required.

A spectacular shot of Hedgehog projectiles leaving the launcher.

In 1940 the Director of Naval Ordnance was made responsible for the development of ahead-throwing weapons and out of this hotch-potch of ideas and meetings came Hedgehog and Squid. The first meeting to regain control of the various projects was held in January 1941. From this point on, it was the Director of Torpedoes and Mines who became the leading light and ensured that projects were co-ordinated. Hedgehog was developed by the Department of Miscellaneous Weapons Development (DMWD), but it had a rival in the

A good image of the landing pattern formed by the Hedgehog projectiles, showing how far ahead of the ship's bow they landed.

Fairlie mortar. The DMWD had suggested using a spigot mortar and this design became Hedgehog.

In some respects, these two weapons superseded the depth charge, though it is still in service at the time of writing. As early as 1939 it was thought that smaller contact charges could damage a U-boat and Hedgehog was a way of delivering many smaller explosive charges, rather than one large one in a depth charge. Describing a Hedgehog bomb as a 'smaller charge' is somewhat misleading since each bomb contained 35lb of explosive with a contact fuze. They were fired from a spigot mounting, with four rows of six projectiles. The bombs would fall in a circle of some 120ft diameter, about 200yd from the ship. Since the bombs were expected to explode on contact, depth was not considered a problem, but it was soon found that Hedgehog was not effective against targets more than 400ft down.

The way the projectiles were fired was interesting. The spigots were spring-loaded. When released by an electrical impulse, they struck the firing case at the base of the projectile, thus firing it. The resultant expanding propellent gases forced the spigot to re-cock itself. Projectiles were fired in pairs in rapid succession. The fit between the spigot and the end of the projectile had to be made with fine tolerances so that the gases did not escape around the spigot. The outstation at Weston-super-Mare was used to test the weapon initially. Although about a hundred ships were fitted with the weapon, it did not receive great acclaim from people who had to use it. Hedgehog has been described in one technical history as 'in no way a development which extended the flexibility of A/S attacks; on the contrary it turned out to be a very fair weather weapon, and when asdic conditions were at all poor the old stern attack was used in preference'.[1]

On one occasion the weapon was a definite threat to the crew and their ship, HMS *Escapade*. They had stopped to assist the frigate *Lagan*, which had just been hit by a torpedo fired from a U-boat. On firing her Hedgehog, the *Escapade* witnessed a massive explosion above the bows. What had happened was that one of the bombs had exploded prematurely when leaving its spigot and it had virtually blown off the vessel's bows, injuring her captain. She still managed to tow the *Lagan* back to Northern Ireland. This is one of the few occasions when this sort of thing happened, but it did not instil confidence in the new weapon in the navy.

Officers continued to prefer the stern attack with depth charges, but this may have been partly unfamiliarity with the new weapons. One thing that came out of the analysis of such attacks was that Hedgehog had not inspired confidence among Royal Navy crews. The depth charge was a terrifying weapon to come up against and a near-miss could be almost as effective as a direct hit. An example of the initial problems with Hedgehog was the battle for Convoy SC 104 in October 1942, which resulted in the loss of eight merchant ships and the destruction of two U-boats. This action was a difficult victory for the Royal Navy.

Group *Wotan* was a unit of ten submarines ordered by U-Boat Command to take up station 300 miles north-east of Newfoundland after refuelling. SC 104 was a convoy of forty-eight merchant ships, which sailed from New York on 3 October. Escort B6 made its rendezvous with the convoy off St John's on 10 October. There were six escort vessels, two British and four Norwegian, the destroyers HMS *Fame* and HMS *Viscount*, and the corvettes *Acanthus*, *Eglantine*, *Montbretia* and *Potentilla*. The destroyers were fitted with Hedgehog as was one Norwegian ship, the *Eglantine*. This battle was fought in lashing rain and pounding seas; often the ASDIC or direction-finding equipment broke down or did not work. At the start, three ships were torpedoed in the convoy and the first attacks by the escorts used gunfire and then ramming – but not Hedgehog.

HMS *Viscount* observed U-607 at short range (800yd) and her captain, Lieutenant Commander John V Waterhouse, fired a pattern of fourteen depth charges set to explode at 50ft and 140ft. When U-607 had reached 60m (200ft), the charges caught her. The depth charges knocked out the U-boat's rudder, depth rudder, depth gauge, compasses, engines and communications systems. The battle raged over 13 and 14 October in seas that were described as Sea State 5. U-618 was also damaged by depth charges. Later in the battle HMS *Viscount* sighted U-661 on the surface and took the opportunity to ram the U-boat behind the conning tower. The destroyer then opened fire with her guns and dropped a single heavy depth charge (a heavy Mark VII probably) alongside the U-boat, which sank with all hands. Apart from the advances in detection, these tactics are reminiscent of attacks in the First World War, even though three of the vessels were armed with Hedgehog! In fact it appears that Hedgehog was not used to any effect and the U-boats were sunk by depth charge, ramming or gunfire.

At a meeting at the Admiralty in February 1942, Squid was conceived. Several projects were conceived at about the same time. The mortar Mark A or Parsnip was being considered and Hedgehog was being produced as well. The scientist B S Smith had developed a mortar at Fairlie, but was not content with the arrangements proposed by the Director of Naval Ordnance, the main problem being that the navy thought the projectiles were too small to be effective. Once again, civilian/naval friction reared its ugly head. This weapon, though, would be almost fully automatic and be a great advance on other concepts.

Parsnip came about because of the problems with Hedgehog. The Parsnip was a further development of the Fairlie mortar designed by Smith's team. Amazingly, these designs appear to have been developed independently of each other. The Fairlie design was the baby of the Anti-submarine branch, whereas the Thornycroft long-range depth-charge thrower was the idea of HMS *Vernon*. The scientist B S Smith at Fairlie protested vociferously against overall control by the Director of Naval Ordnance and the feud was resolved only when Smith was removed in 1942.

Parsnip was made up of two steel units, each containing ten barrels. The whole unit was mounted in a cradle, supported on two bearings. The rear bearing was designed to take the thrust of the recoil. The units were placed to port and starboard and the projectiles fell in a semicircular pattern, because the barrels were all set at different angles. As with the later Squid, the Parsnip was electrically fired and used a cartridge-and-breech arrangement for the propellant. The cradles could be wound to horizontal for loading, and firing was carried out in pairs of barrels with a delay of 0.1 seconds between each pair. A single barrel was tested at Thornycroft in Woolston; pattern trials were carried out on board HMS *Ambuscade*; and sea trials were completed in February 1943.

Squid was a three-barrelled mortar that fired a particularly large projectile, which weighed 400lb and contained 200lb of explosive. According to Willem Hackmann, 'Its most novel feature was the automatic setting of the depth pistols of the projectiles by the Type 147 depth-determining asdic set'.[2] The three barrels were set at a fixed elevation, but mounted at their base on a horizontal training axis driven by a motor. This could alter the training angle by about 30° side to side. The three barrels were fixed slightly out of alignment so that when fired the bombs would land in a triangular pattern of about 120ft on each side. Unlike Hedgehog, Squid was able to explode its charges at varying depths and, if a ship were armed with two weapons, they could be arranged to fire at different depths.

Squid was revolutionary because it was developed in conjunction with a depth-measuring ASDIC unit. The projectiles had time fuzes, which were set automatically when the depth of the target was known. The sinking speed was expected to be 40ft per second. The body had a flat nose and rounded front end, but otherwise it was cylindrical, terminating in a stabilizing tail. The nose was weighted by being made from cast iron. Gas checks were built into the body. The fuze was set into the nose and had a two-stage arming device, which was initiated on set-back in the mortar ('set-back' being the term for the shock transmitted to the fuze when the projectile is launched) and fully armed on impact when it entered the water. These two features were combined with an altered clock-timed mechanical fuze, number 211 Mark 3. These devices were chosen because they were already in production and available in quantity. The technical history produced by the department explained the workings of the mechanical fuze:

> the mechanism, when started, continues to run until the 'hand' reaches a form recess in the hand race, the position of which has been preset by the setting motor actuated by electrical impulses transmitted from the Depth Setting Control (DSC) in the ASDIC room in accordance with the last depth prediction. Firing occurs when the hand is ejected into the recess in the present position.[3]

This weapon did not come into service until 1943 but it quickly had an impact. For example, on 6 March 1944 in the North Atlantic, Canadian convoy support group C2 chased the German type-VIIC submarine U-744, commanded by *Oberleutnant* Heinz Blischke. U-744 had been hunted for 32 hours, since 10.00 on the previous day, and the crew were exhausted from the sustained effort and weak from oxygen deprivation. Combination attacks with depth charges and Squid anti-submarine mortars had damaged the pressure hull, the air purifiers and the diesel engines. The boat was forced to the surface where it was riddled by gunfire, from HMCS *Chilliwack* and *Fennel*, and was forced to surrender.

In July 1944, U-333 was destroyed to the west of the Scilly Islands by the sloop *Starling* and the frigate HMS *Loch Killin* of the 2nd Escort Group using the new Squid to fire three of the large projectiles. This was the first confirmed destruction of a U-boat with this ahead-throwing anti-submarine weapon. Much of its development had been carried out at Leigh Park. Squid was far superior to Hedgehog and the depth charge, and soon established a 50 per cent kill rate. In comparison the depth charge had a 12 per cent likelihood of destroying a U-boat. By the end of the war, sixty to seventy Squid had been fitted to escort vessels and they continued in service after 1945. Improvements in the projectile were a low priority, only carried out after the war, since the effectiveness of aircraft attacks had proved sufficient in 1943.

Cloak and dagger

HMS *Vernon* (M) was not confined to working on purely naval weapons. As invasion of Europe drew closer, it was increasingly involved in preparing secret weapons. Back in July 1940 the department had been devising anti-invasion devices such as demolition charges and evaluating commercial explosives and detonators. The use of demolition explosives by naval forces ashore was considered important and by October 1940 many had been developed and supplied to the navy, and could be adapted for use in the 1944 invasion of France.

Even early in the war, when anti-invasion devices were being prepared, more staff were needed: a Royal Naval Volunteer Reserve officer was added to the establishment, as well as several warrant officers for assisting with experiments. After a great deal of trial and error, the department found that most commercially available demolition explosives were unusable for military work and recommended a new series of primers, fuzes and explosive charges, mainly based on amatol fillings. It is striking that the Mark VII depth charge was considered as a demolition charge! In this guise a detonator adaptor was developed so that, instead of a pistol, it had an electrical or cordtex detonator fitted to the charge via a watertight gland. This sort of device became invaluable in the clearance of harbours and installations of mines, especially from early 1944.

The Second World War saw further development of explosives and two in particular should be mentioned: RDX and Torpex. RDX was about 30 to 50 per cent more powerful than TNT and was unstable. It was a trinitro compound, further improved by adding aluminium. This increased the heat of combustion and the blast effect. Torpex was used after 1943 in many torpedo warheads and mine explosive chambers as their main filling.

The following weapons were developed at least in part by HMS *Vernon* (M):

- Chariots copied the Italian two-man submarine and were used to lay charges under warships in harbour and blow them up: *Vernon* ensured that the warhead was powerful enough to do the job.
- X-craft: staff at Leigh Park House and *Vernon* designed the side charges.
- Boom-patrol boats, with their complex system of detonation.
- Counter-mining weapons called Hedgerow and Bookrest, intended for the clearance of beach mines.

In the case of the boom-patrol boats, the name was deliberately misleading: they were meant not to patrol booms, but simply to go 'boom'. Intended for use by the Royal Marines, the concept was effectively an explosive motor boat. In December 1941, the Italians had crippled the cruiser HMS *York* and the idea was to attack their warships in the same way. The explosive charge of 500lb was carried in the bow and it could be fired in three different ways. The first was by hydrostatic detonation: the boat was scuttled, so she would sink and explode at a pre-determined depth. The second method was a time fuze, by which the boat could be destroyed at a pre-determined moment. Finally, the boat would explode on impact with the target. All of these operations were to be initiated electrically.

An interesting phenomenon began to develop as the invasion of Europe began to loom. HMS *Vernon* (M) began to develop a reputation, not just for the expertise of its staff, but as an organization that could get things done. The Department of Torpedoes and Mines was no longer the only organization using *Vernon*. The Chief of Combined Operations required demolition charges as early as 1941, and the Commander-in-Chief Portsmouth and Flag Officer Submarines required more esoteric devices to continue the war effort. This pointed to a widening of the role of the unit's scientists and engineers. The commander of *Vernon* stated that the facility concentrated on the following technical issues during the middle of the Second World War:

- Introduction of aircraft-laid depth charges;
- Ahead-throwing weapons;
- Improvements in surface-launched depth charges;
- Introduction of demolition explosives, assault weapons and accessories;
- Cloak-and-dagger assistance;
- Compilation of handbooks for various weapon systems.

One tactic the Germans tried at the end of 1943 was the use of midget submarines and human torpedoes. The *Biber* and *Neger* were dangerous weapons. The latter was a converted G7e electric torpedo, with another such weapon slung underneath it. The warhead of the 'mother ship' was modified to accommodate the controls and the pilot sat beneath the plexiglass dome and steered the *Neger* towards a target. When within range, the pilot would start the baby's motor and send it on its run. These weapons were intended to attack the Italian and Normandy invasion fleets. To combat them, *Vernon* introduced the Mark XII depth charge, which was smaller and intended for use from coastal force vessels. It entered service in May 1943 and was immediately successful.

Depth charges were being adapted for all sorts of uses and the lateral thinking that accompanied their use seemed to have no limits. There was even a system for using them from a harbour. This was called the AMUCK or the rocket-propelled depth charge. It was a very strange beast indeed and consisted of a depth charge, mounted on a metal rack made by Rubery Owen & Co. of Darlaston, Staffordshire, surrounded by twelve 2-inch rocket motors to project it into the air. The rocket motors came from the air-launched rocket. The Director of Underwater Weapons stated: 'Trials showed that the method of projection was not entirely satisfactory due to the possibility of a misfire, or late ignition, of one, or more, of the rockets. The resulting asymmetry of thrust could produce dangerous errors of range and line.'[4]

The last year of war for HMS *Vernon* continued to be a fight to the death. Although U-boats had effectively been defeated in the Battle of the Atlantic in 1943, the use of the *Schnorkel* made them much more difficult to detect. Under these circumstances it became less clear what the U-boat command would do; they began to attack the shipping that supplied Allied forces in Europe to try to break their supply lines. The general opinion was that the ahead-throwing weapons such as Hedgehog and Squid accounted for a fair number of U-boat losses but 'the larger part of the kills were still due to the much larger number of depth-charge attacks'.[5] There is no doubt that the combination of aircraft and the Mark XI depth charge made a very significant change to the war against the U-boat. Constant improvements in reliability and delivery mechanisms rendered depth charges a most potent weapon against the U-boat threat.

One factor that tended to cloud the ability of ships to attack submarines was the question of automatic firing. The Squid launching system was automatic and relied on the ASDIC set to trigger it once the calculations had been made. The ability to launch at just the right moment depended on the type of ship and how up-to-date it was. Visual indicators were common and were relatively trouble-free once installed. However, they meant that heavy reliance was placed upon the crew, and their ability to maintain drill and discipline under very difficult conditions, and this fact was widely acknowledged by the staff at *Vernon*.

We have already seen that Hedgehog was one of the ahead-throwing weapons used to combat the U-boat in 1943–4, but its use was not limited to the destruction of U-boats. The invasion of Europe was at last being considered in 1943 and the thoughts of Allied commanders turned to the obstacles they would have to overcome. Of all the weapons that would cause problems on the beaches, the mine was one of the more complicated to overcome. A combination of sea mines and land mines blocked the likely invasion beaches. The Germans had laid thousands of Teller mines and these caused concern. In October 1942 the Hedgehog bomb was considered as a way of dealing with mines and the project was codenamed Hedgerow. Most of the direction and co-ordination of the project was shared between the Director of the Department of Miscellaneous Weapons Development and the Road Research Laboratory.

The idea was that converted landing craft could be used to launch Hedgehog bombs at the beachhead and clear a path through the mines. It had been calculated that the German mines would be buried $3\frac{1}{2}$in below the sand. Tests with TNT-filled Hedgehog bombs proved unsuccessful, so a more powerful combination of RDX and TNT was next used. Trials were carried out on Berrow Flats at Weston-super-Mare in February and March 1943, to see how effective the Hedgehog rounds were against the Teller mine as well as the distance at which they would affect the German mines. It was also intended to find out how deep Mark IV mines had to be buried to get the same effect. Finally the use of RDX and TNT needed to be proved. Previously the bombs had been fitted with contact fuzes, intended to go off on contact with a submarine's hull. Now the weapons were to clear a path 120yd long by 8yd wide through a minefield, about 100yd ahead of the landing craft they were mounted in. Their salvo was elliptical and the throwers needed to be aligned in two straight lines for this to happen. The existing launching mount also needed to be fitted with a different kind of fuze to be effective.

The very first Hedgerow was fitted on LCT 162 Mark II. There were actually three types of mounting in the Hedgerow: Mark I, Mark II* and Mark II* converted. The bombs were mounted on a spigot, which was in turn fixed to an I-beam. The bomb had an elongated contact fuze, extended forward of the main charge, which was increased in size. Each spigot had a slightly different elevation because it was calculated that each bomb would follow a linear dispersed trajectory. Hedgerow was fitted to LCAs, which had to be strengthened to withstand the firing of the weapon, as well as to LCTs. In June 1943 new contracts were placed with Thomson Brothers of Bilston for 25 Hedgerow Mark II mountings and some modifications were made. The Mark II* mounting had alterations to the round and the spigots, which had different angles. Ready-made sockets were made for the new angles; these were added to the original mounts and called Mark II* converted. Most were converted at Portsmouth, Chatham or Rosyth, and the rest by the firm of Thornycroft, which always seemed to be involved with such work.[6]

Bookrest was another counter-mining project where the talents of the *Vernon* team were used – in this case, to discover how best to clear beach mines buried in the sand. Bookrest was basically a hose filled with explosive, carried into a minefield by either a line thrower or a rocket. The idea was that the hose could then be detonated and the mines would go with it thus clearing a path through which a tank could drive. Tests were carried out in 1945 in which German Teller mines, type TMI 42, were tested to see if the idea would work. A 100ft hose was buried 2–4in in the sand, in a minefield with the nearest mines buried 2ft from the hose. The results were disappointing and the project was not pursued.[7]

So one of these projects was successful and the other was a failure: only Hedgerow was used in anger. In Operation Overlord, two flotillas of landing craft fitted with Hedgerow were used in the assault. Royal Marine crews manned them, but the vagaries of the weather put paid to a perfect assault. The unfortunate Flotilla 592 lost all but one of its nine vessels on the way over, but LCA 976 did fire its Hedgerow. Flotillas 590 and 591, of eighteen vessels each, were involved in the attack.

In Flotilla 590 ten vessels fired at the target, one of which sank, perhaps because of the strain put upon it by firing the weapon! Four arrived too late and three didn't make the passage. In Flotilla 591 nine fired and nine were lost on passage. It seems that twenty vessels sank because they were not seaworthy enough to make the trip. This does suggest that the LCA was not really suitable for the task involved and just under half the force could not be used to good effect. Comments from those who saw Hedgerow in action emphasize that it was actually very effective in clearing minefields. It proved the value of a lot of this experimental work when it finally became a success with the end-user.

Chapter Eleven
X-craft and their charges

One of the great successes of the Italian Navy was its inspired use of the manned torpedo and the midget submarine: with the right approach a few men could immobilize a capital ship. It was not until the Royal Navy had lost several large vessels that they began to take the midget submarine seriously. The result was two of the great British underwater successes of the Second World War, the X-craft and the Chariot. After initial discussions between the army and navy, a requirement was defined for a midget underwater submarine. The X-craft, about 50ft long and with a crew of three (or four in later models), was a diminutive but deadly weapon in the right hands. Their subsequent success against the German battleship *Tirpitz* earned their crews everlasting fame. Daring underwater attacks by a few men against heavily guarded capital ships are rare, and rarely fully successful.

If the *Tirpitz* had been their only success, that would probably be enough, but X-craft were also used as reconnaissance craft for the D-day landings and

The explosive side charges for the X-craft. This view shows the interior, the side that connected to the submarine.

in attacks on German-held dock installations in Norway. The story of the craft in themselves is a long and tortuous tale and really belongs to the story of submarine construction. It is enough to say that the idea was taken over from the army in 1940 and the project was put under the control of the Director of Naval Construction. Commander C H Varley DSC, who owned his own engineering works, was one of the prime movers in the enterprise and certainly claimed from the Admiralty that the X-craft were his idea. This was bending the truth a little, because the concept of midget submarines was not new.

Two prototypes were built, X3 and X4, but it was X5–X10, the boats manufactured by Vickers, that were to be used to attack the *Tirpitz*. Further attack craft were built at Broadbents, including two other versions: the XT, without charges and used for training purposes, and the XE, a special development for the Far East. The XE boats were expected to encounter unusually high humidity and therefore were given different electrical systems. The construction of the vessels is not part of this story, but their weapons are. The X-craft carried no torpedoes, but were designed to lay explosive charges underneath their victims. These were known as side charges because they were fixed to the side of the submarine. The side charge itself went through a number of incarnations before it was ready for use. Each was eventually to weigh two tons (4,480lb). The explosive element was amatol, a nitro–glycerine-based explosive similar to TNT. Amatol did not always explode completely and so the final mark of charge, the Mark XX, contained amatex. For clarification it is worth noting that in 1943 TNT was replaced by torpex, which was much more powerful. The combination of torpex with amatol became known as amatex.

The side charges themselves had to meet several requirements. The first was to blow up when required. It was a worthless exercise to train and potentially sacrifice a number of valuable naval personnel if at the last moment their weapon did not function. The explosive had to be powerful enough to break the back of a large vessel and it had to be able to withstand the water pressure on its metal casing. In addition, when the charges were dropped they had to sink to the bottom and not float. This meant that the casing had to have free-flooding ballast chambers, so they would sink rapidly.

Exterior view of the side-charge casing.

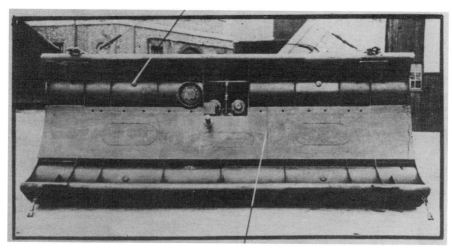

Another view of the heavily constructed casing, built to withstand the depth at which the X-craft was likely to lay its charge.

Finally an explosive initiator had to be used that gave the crew enough time to get away from the scene before it exploded and so a good time-operated fuze was needed.

The side charges for the X-craft were not easily produced and nothing as large as two tons of explosive had been tried on a midget submarine. The Office of Admiral (Submarines) reported on 15 June 1943:

> The clock fuse and the side charges generally were the one remaining technical uncertainty of the X-craft, and of course the culminating factor for which the craft were designed.[1]

The shadow of Herbert Taylor appears again in this story because it seems he was involved in the design of these weapons. Only one document has been discovered that links Taylor with the X-craft side charges; frustratingly, it only hints at his part in their development. His final letter of retirement mentions his involvement with them, which is confirmed by oral evidence of people who worked at the site. We do know that a secret unit known as K section, at Leigh Park House, was responsible for their design and this unit was linked with Taylor. It must also be remembered that his son was working on the site at the time, though mostly on depth-charge pistols. Some confusion is understandable since staff were not always sure what other parts of the organization were doing.

One person who worked at West Leigh, and was kind enough to write down his memories and give them to the author, was David Clark. He recalled that a colleague of his was working in a small workshop at HMS *Vernon* during the

MK. 20 CHARGE CASE

MECHANISM PLATE, MK.19.

BUOYANCY TANK No.2
WITH END FAIRING.

TEAK RUBBING
STREAK (TO FAIR OFF
FILLING HOLES.

The Mark 20 case with buoyancy fairing.

Mark 22 explosive charge case for limpet mines, used on board the X-craft.

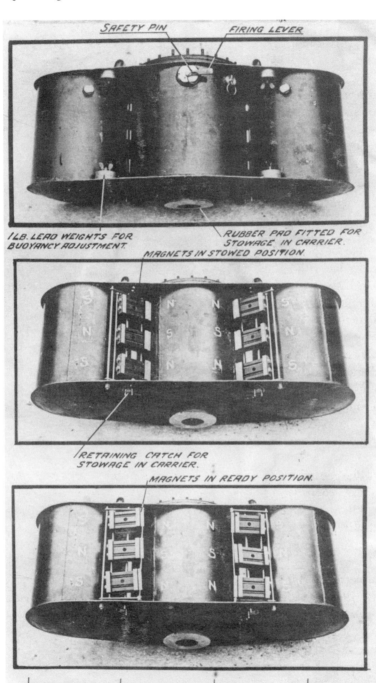

An exterior view of the Mark 22.

early part of 1943. This team, probably K section, was working on electrical circuit assemblies for fitting to ground-laid mines. He adds:

> I later discovered that these assemblies, of which there were many different circuit types, were prepared in small numbers as required for specific operations, e.g. different sensitivities, different arming periods, different lifetime (two to six months), some to catch small vessels, some to catch minesweepers etc. I believe this was K section.[2]

In 1944 a similar team was in evidence at West Leigh, working on similar assemblies to be used for mines that were to interdict shipping for D-Day. They may be the same department. It is likely that this department was responsible for the design of the charges. The X-craft side charge was in effect a ground mine with a timer and so it would have made sense to use people on the project who were familiar with this type of device.

Alan Pilledge, who was mentioned earlier, has this to say about charge development:

> Very early on, I recall having to test the time delay mechanism of the charges which were dropped by X-craft, the midget submarines. This was a simple dashpot but filled with grease instead of oil. I presume it was hoped that grease would be less liable than oil to leak away in such a situation. It was a crude device but then timers (other than clocks) were pretty primitive at that time.[3]

Mr Pilledge goes on to say that the charges were certainly designed up at Leigh Park House, where Taylor was seen coming and going – but then so were many others. The operation at Leigh Park House and West Leigh had expanded beyond all expectations and many famous scientists were drafted into the organization. They seem to have moved about, working on different projects, and it is possible they were involved in explosive tests. The sheer breadth of their projects and the nature of their work go way beyond the scope of this book. By 1944 a large team of scientists and engineers had been marshalled to deal with any sort of operation from air-dropped mines to submarine weapons to depth charges. The old days of a few people in one or two small workshops were, like the First World War, a distant memory.

The side charges, fitted to midget submarine X7, were tested by the 12th Submarine Flotilla. HMS *Thrasher* towed the X7 to Ardmaleish, on Bute, where technicians from Vickers-Armstrong and Messrs Graseby fitted the firing mechanisms, in part to demonstrate to ships' officers, principally from HMS *Bonaventure*, how it was done. The X7 was towed to Loch Cairnbawn (code HHZ), in the far north-west of Scotland, and dived to 150ft to make sure that the charges withstood the depth. In fact, water leaked into the firing mechanisms. This led the trial officers to decide that the clock time should be set on leaving harbour, so the charges would go off at a specific time after departure. This seems somewhat restrictive, especially if unexpected events occurred on a sortie, as they often did. It was also decided to add painted canvas covers to the master units used for setting the clock. Both charges were laid in 23 fathoms (138ft) of water, with an interval of 15min and 400yd between them, the port charge 50ft down and the starboard 55ft down. The subsequent splash of the explosion was 132ft high and 600ft wide.[4] The officer in charge expressed his dissatisfaction at the time, complaining they had only killed six fish in the process!

If the British made good use of midget submarines such as the X-craft, they were shown the way by the Italians, who were the arch-exponents of the manned torpedo or *Maiale*, as they called it. Officially named the SLC or *Siluro a Lenta Corsa*, the two-man torpedo operated by the *Decima Mas* naval unit proved to be a thorn in the side of the Royal Navy. The battleships *Queen Elizabeth* and *Valiant* were damaged severely by the Italians and this form of attack was seriously considered and eventually authorized by the Royal Navy. Their first Chariot was tested in June 1942. Again the warhead is the part we are interested in and it came about as part of the design efforts of the team at Leigh Park House.

Commander C H Varley had come up with an idea for a midget submarine in 1939, but it was the Italians who led the way. The Director of Naval Contracts, the Flag Officer Submarines and HMS *Vernon* (M) all contributed to the project. In effect the Chariot was a manned torpedo. It was the 21-inch torpedo with a position for two men astride it, facing forward. One man guided the vessel and controlled it while the other carried out the demolition work. It was electrically powered and designed to take a 600lb warhead. In all, sixty Mark I Chariots were built by Stothard and Pitt, who also built twenty-three Mark IIs for £120,000.

The Mark II Chariot was a move away from the design of the Mark I, in that the two crew sat back to back. The warhead could not be like a conventional torpedo warhead, because of the way it would be deployed, so the Navy had to look to other solutions. Effectively the charge was designed to be slung underneath the target. The two operators or divers were expected to wear closed-cycle diving suits, which left no tell-tale air bubbles on the surface because they recycled their oxygen. They had to fix their charges onto the target ship by two or four magnetic clamps, from which the warhead was suspended on cables.

H Smith, in *True Stories of World War Two*, recounting the attack on the Italian cruiser *Bolzano* in La Spezia in 1943, recalled: 'Together we placed four magnets on the bottom of the ship, releasing the warhead of the torpedo, and lashed it to the magnets.' When all was secure, the warhead was disengaged from the Chariot by unscrewing a central bolt that ran through the warhead, using a handwheel. This operation was risky and awkward, as the weight of the warhead affected the balance of the Chariot. It may have occurred to the reader that a 600lb warhead would be a difficult thing to handle under water, even if its weight in water was much less. In order to make it acceptable, the warhead was provided with buoyancy devices. The warhead itself relied on a timer and normally this would be set to allow the operators several hours to get well away.

On 18 November 1942, the Superintendent of Mine Design wrote to the Director of Torpedoes and Mines to express his satisfaction at the testing of the Chariot Mark II warhead. A new warhead had been detonated, suspended 30ft below the surface and containing 533lb of Minol I. (Service warheads contained 1,140lb of torpex and would be much more powerful.) The explosion was truly spectacular and forced sprays of water hundreds of feet into the air.[5] This type was to be attached to the submarine via four clips around the base of the warhead. There was a great deal of discussion of this attachment, as in this note from the Captain of the 5th Submarine Flotilla to the Admiral Submarines:

1. The release gear was at the after end of the head so that the operator does not lose contact with the Chariot when the head is released.
2. It can be worked with one hand leaving the other free for holding on, which is one of the first principles of diving.
3. The head construction was simplified as the central rod and tube was no longer required.[6]

The new design was far more sensible, since it was easier to handle. It relied on three mine Mark XIA primers and a Mark V firing mechanism. The head itself was made of non-magnetic steel, weighed 1,730lb and contained 1,140lb of torpex. To balance the warhead in the water, a series of lead weights could be hung on it, so it could be trimmed in situ.

The X-craft were used successfully against several targets. Apart from the attack on the *Tirpitz*, they were to be used to sink the SS *Baranfels* as it lay alongside a floating dock at Laksvaag, near Bergen, Norway. This attack damaged the dock and coaling facilities. The Laksvaag dock used by the Germans was destroyed in a later raid. One of the most spectacular attacks was the destruction of the Japanese cruiser *Takao* in Singapore Harbour on 31 July 1945.

The link between midget submarines and HMS *Vernon* (M) trials did not stop at the Chariot and the X-craft. The Special Operations Executive (SOE) were interested in such vessels, because they were seen as the ideal vehicle for infiltrating the enemy coast. One such scheme involved a weird creature called the Welman craft. Colonel John Dolphin of the Royal Engineers invented this electrically powered one-man submarine with a detachable warhead, a concept not dissimilar to the Chariot. The Welman craft, though, was fully enclosed and the pilot sat in a small conning tower in the middle. Never has something so small relied on so many borrowed bits and pieces, taking the joystick from a Spitfire and the seat from an Austin 7 car, which will give some idea of how the craft was cobbled together. In 1942 the Welman's development was well under way, but SOE decided to give it up as a bad job and the navy were saddled with the unwanted responsibility of doing something with it.

Enter HMS *Vernon* (M), whose job it was to develop the warhead. They came up with the goods after quite a bit of experimentation and the result was a far better solution than that originally conceived for the Chariot Mark I. The weapon was 31in in diameter, 4ft long and weighed in total 540kg. It contained the charge case mark XIV and used 403–460lb of explosive. As with the Chariot warheads, it had positive buoyancy of 10lb. The warhead had ten powerful magnets in two rows. The idea was that the Welman craft was positioned under the enemy ship, the warhead magnets were offered up to the ship's hull and the warhead was released from the boat by a securing screw inside the vessel. Better than that, the positive buoyancy forced the magnets against the ship hull.

When the craft was reversed away, the explosive timer started to work automatically, actuating a clockwork firing device. Why this wasn't thought of earlier is a bit of a mystery, because all descriptions of early Chariot attacks suggest that positioning the warhead was a long-winded and difficult process. There was, however, one big difficulty with the magnetic attachment method: fouling of the ship's hull had not been taken into account. Growths on the hull would weaken the connection and render the magnets almost useless. On more than one occasion the Chariot divers had to find other ways of securing the charge. In addition to the features discussed above, the Welman warhead had an anti-firing device, whereby the charge once placed could not be removed without firing it. Nevertheless the Welman warhead was a well-designed device and it was a pity the rest of the craft was not so well thought out. It was nowhere near as successful as the X-craft.

Chapter Twelve

Conclusion

The depth charge was one of the most important anti-submarine weapons of the twentieth century, but the question of its early effectiveness is somewhat vexing. I have tried to show that at first depth charges were variable in their effects, they were sometimes unreliable and the early designs were only a small gain on the explosive charges previously used. But in that critical year of 1917 their wider use and their crippling effect on morale showed their value, and the investment began to pay dividends in 1918, the last year of the First World War.

The mine, in a series of parallel developments, was not only a deadly anti-submarine weapon but was just as dangerous, if not more so, to surface ships. It is worth remembering just how big a programme the mining effort was in both world wars. In the Second World War British ships and aircraft laid approximately 206,000 buoyant mines and 57,000 ground mines. It is thought that they sank or damaged 1,588 vessels, unarguably a large figure. In effect, this meant that 156 mines were laid for each vessel damaged.[1]

On Herbert Taylor's retirement in 1945, Captain F H N Vaughn RN presented him with a decorative scroll containing an expression of gratitude from his colleagues. He retired to his main hobbies of gardening and motoring. Taylor died in 1957 and was buried in Warblington Cemetery in Hampshire, where his grave is still marked by an unassuming headstone in a row of similar stones. For such a prodigious inventor, his passing was quietly celebrated in the naval journals of the time. His story is like that of many others who served their country by their remarkable response to the constantly shifting and sliding technical requirements of the Royal Navy's life-or-death struggle. But, in the author's view, Taylor represented more than that.

Herbert Taylor represented the 'can do' spirit of an age of inventors. He constantly came up with new ideas or modifications to improve naval weapons or reduce their cost. If one looks at photographs of trials or workshops, especially in the two world wars, it becomes evident that working in 'the department' brought little glory. The work was heavy engineering mostly, with a degree of ever-present danger from the explosive charges. It was dirty, it was carried on in all weathers and it relied on monotonous tests that were often carried out in the most inhospitable places. It was possible to be killed while experimenting, but this does not seem to have entered people's minds at the time.

The reverse side of the medal was that it was possible, though unlikely, that one might benefit from an invention by patenting it or getting recognition from the Admiralty for one's efforts. There is a certain duality about making weapons of war that kill people and taking financial gain from that. Taylor possibly made something in the region of £30,000 from Vickers from his designs and this was a colossal amount of money then. He was eventually recognized by the government as an important engineer and was awarded the MBE.

In parallel with Taylor, we see glimpses of many more, similar characters who were seemingly capable of applying themselves to any kind of mechanical or electrical engineering problem – R A Sturgeon, D Burney, A L Gwynne, A B Wood, J G D Ouvry, H L Skipworth – all involved in the constant technical battle against our naval enemies. Quite a lot has been written about the scientists who were involved in technical development in the Second World War and so I have not focused on them here. Much, too, has been written about certain departments and sections, those dealing with encryption and radar, for instance, but there is no doubt that many more contributed to the new weapons and equipment meant to counter the Axis threat. All those outstations, staffed by talented but largely unknown and unsung specialists, were needed. In the Second World War, new weapons were introduced or developed at a quite extraordinary rate compared to the First World War. It is easy to see why a small department based in a warehouse in 1914 could become a large organization by 1945. Yet it was still made up of individuals, engaged in a scientific war against German, Italy and Japan.

The reason for singling out the individuals in the First World War is because they can be singled out. More than any others, Taylor and Gwynne can be identified as the people who invented one of the most potent anti-submarine weapons of the twentieth century. By the Second World War, they had been subsumed into a much larger and more flexible machine. Nevertheless, that machine still relied on one particular individual whose specialist knowledge was fully exploited. By his unique abilities and experience, Herbert Taylor had become 'the guru of the depth-charge pistol', as one of his contemporaries called him.[2]

The question of technical co-operation between the United States and the United Kingdom in the First World War is a difficult one. On one hand the Admiralty was very keen to help the Americans establish an effective anti-submarine fleet. The war after Jutland was almost exclusively a war against merchant shipping on the part of the Germans, and therefore it became an anti-submarine war on the British side. Both Fullinwider and Minckler used ideas supplied by the Royal Navy. There is no question of this if the adjudication of the Patents Office of the United States is to be accepted. It is also clear that the Admiralty clearly stated that the patents of the mechanisms supplied, and the rights of their inventors, were not to be prejudiced. Yet within a very short time members of the United States Bureau of Ordnance had patented them.

The question remains whether the United States Government was aware of this at the time. It would seem highly unlikely that they were not aware of it, considering the crucial need for weapons development at that time. It may be that they turned a blind eye to the private patenting of the items to ensure that the United States had the best naval technology available. Further research may well reveal if this is the case.

If necessity is the mother of invention, then war is the accelerator of invention. In his book *The Paravane Adventure*, L Cope-Cornford stated that he had received some criticism for singling out the history of the Paravane Department from among others, as an important contribution to the prosecution of the war. The Admiralty objected by stating that "the narrative ignores throughout every other factor which made for the defeat of the submarine and the mine". I am happy to follow his convention and say that I have not covered every aspect of the two world wars, because it was the history and effect of the depth charge and the mine that I was interested in and that is what I have tried to deal with here.

One factor that rarely gets a mention in books on inventors and their ideas is the fact that the men with the ideas were set to gain financially from them. This in itself is not unusual, but it does throw into doubt the often accepted idea that inventors and producers were all selflessly working together to win the war. This was often not the case. In fact, all the naval officers and engineers involved in these developments were keen to benefit financially from their ideas. Perhaps Dennis Burney was the exception, but it is difficult to say for sure. The themes that run through this book – individual invention or group effort, national survival or personal gain – touch on motives so complex that it is difficult to believe that anything would have been achieved at all except by pandering to ego or greed.

At the same time, Britain's naval hierarchy and questions of status and influence muddied the waters, in a way that no mine ever did. People like Herbert Taylor were at once elevated but also enlightened by their experiences, but recognition and reward came belatedly and grudgingly. This meant they were unable to recognize that their lives and opportunities had been enhanced, albeit by forces that they had no way of controlling.

In this book I hope to have raised people's awareness of characters who contributed greatly to the improvement of naval weapons and therefore to the survival of the nation as a whole. More importantly, I hope to have added another small piece to the jigsaw puzzle of the histories of the First and Second World Wars. Whether I have achieved this is entirely up to the reader to decide.

Appendix

Herbert Taylor's inventions

These are designs claimed by Taylor to have been invented solely by him.

Depth charges
C-type Depth Charge
C*-type Depth-Charge Pistol
C-type Primer
D-, D*- and G-type Depth-Charge Pistol Mark I and II (Patent Application No. 8929/16)
D-type Depth-Charge Pistol Mark III and V*
E*-type Depth-Charge Pistol
E-type Embodied Pistol
Primer Safety Gear for Depth Charge Mark I and II (Patent Application Nos 2928/16, 2929/16)
Primer Safety Gear Mark V for depth charges used in throwers (Patent Application No. 1526/17)
Float M Pistol (Patent Application No. 8929/16)
Hydrostatic Release Type I and II (Patent Application No. 8929/16)

Sinkers
Type K (Mark XIV), designed to meet requirements of depths from 100–1000 fathoms (600–6,000ft) for above-water laying
S, Type C (Mark XVI), for submarine laying
Hydrostatic anchor release, replaced the original mechanical release on the K sinker for above-water laying, provided with a leak hole to give delay; used on the P type sinker
Hydrostat Mark VII, adapted for use on the SV mine

Mines
Mine H, Type G, for above-water laying with sinker Type K and detachable charge case of 500lb or 320lb
Mine S, Type B, for submarine laying with Sinker B, Type C detachable charge case of 320lb

Mine H, Type H, barrel-belted mine designed for high buoyancy
Mechanism plate type L, for use with Mine H, Type G
Mechanism plate type M, for use with Mine S, Type B
Detonator release type A
Detonator release type B
Mine horn Mark IV, a small but important improvement on the Hertz horn, it
  was far more robust and relied on a simple switch operated by a ball-and-
  socket movement; subsequently used on many different types of British
  mines
Dashpot for SI and SII mine
Dashpot for SV mine
Holder and wedge for cutter wires (Patent Application No. 12777/16)

Additional ancillary objects
Clock electric type C, an internal clock design for up to 40 days' operation,
  providing an accurate timing device unaffected by temperature and of use
  when a mine had been laid
Flooder type N
Relay type C
AC switch type E
Depth-taking gear
Primer M type B
Switch horns type A and B
Relay type E
Taylor also found time to carry out trials on other forms of naval ordnance
equipment that didn't actually make it into service.

Sinkers
S Type A 80 fathoms (480ft)
Type N 100–1,000 fathoms (600–6,000ft)
Type P 80 fathoms (480ft)
Type S Fixed mooring
Simple sinker 200 fathoms (1,200ft)

Mines
Ground Mine M Type C, 1,000lb explosive with two magnetic CR rods – six
  were produced but were not required by the Admiralty
Mine H, Type K, an anti-minesweeping device
Smoke mine – several were produced and tried but not adopted
Mine CR F, a compound mine with CR and contacts, which was renamed the
  C-type J

This is just a small sample of the list of devices that Taylor was involved in and
demonstrates his considerable inventiveness.

Bibliography

Primary sources
Explosion: Museum of Naval Firepower Archive and Priddy's Hard Archive, Winchester Records Office
Annual Report of HMS *Vernon*, 1892–1918 (26 volumes)
'A History of the Naval Ordnance Inspectorate' by W Stillgate, 1951 [unpublished: copy at Explosion! The Museum of Naval Firepower]
PH2002.1355 – Personal papers of Herbert Taylor
Superintendent Armament Supply Officer, Priddy's Hard, memorandum for inclusion in Technical History in regard to storage of ammunition and development of depots, Priddy's Hard, 30 January 1919 (Priddy's Hard Museum Archive)
Proceedings of the Ordnance Committee, 1927–45
BR 1669 (1)–(6) Depth-charge technical manuals
BR 1063 Depth-charge Pocket Book, Torpedo and Mining Department, 1944

Naval Historical Branch, Portsmouth
Italian depth-charge manuals, German technical manuals and HMS *Vernon* evaluations of the weapons of other navies

Royal Navy Submarine Archive, Gosport, Hampshire
A1944/002, A1938/002, A1977/061, A1930/001, A1992/101, A2000/363
'List of German submarines sunk on operations during World War One' (revd Sep. 1987)

National Archives (formerly the Public Records Office), Kew, London
Documents ADM 199/1175, ADM 1/13941, ADM 1/14811, TS 32/87, ADM 1/25246, TS 27/753, ADM 189/99, ADM 186/368, ADM 1/12522

Patent Office, London
Patents 247,695; 157,997; 277,385; 277,386; 295,145; 295,586; 163,340

Author's collection
Personal memories of West Leigh employees David Clark and Alan Pilledge, in letters and e-mails

Secondary sources
Armstrong, Sir George Elliot, bart, *Torpedoes and Torpedo-Vessels, etc.*, Bell & Sons: London, 1901
Beevor, A, *Crete: The battle and the resistance*, Penguin: London, 1991
Bennett, G M, *Naval Battles of the First World War*, Penguin: London, 2001
Brennecke, J, *The Hunter and the Hunted*, Burke: London, 1958
Buchheim, L G, *U-boat War*, Collins: London, 1978
Busch, H, *U-boats at War*, Putnam: London, 1955
Campbell, N J M, *Naval Weapons of World War Two*, Conway Maritime Press: London, 1985
Cope-Cornford, L, *The Paravane Adventure*, Hodder & Stoughton: London, 1919
Cowie, J S, Mines, *Minelayers and Minesweeping*, OUP: Oxford, 1951
Director of Underwater Weapons, 'Technical history of anti-submarine weapons', Director of Underwater Weapons Departmental, 24 February 1950
Dommett, W E, *Submarine Vessels: including mines, torpedoes, guns, steering, propelling and navigating apparatus: and with notes on submarine offensive and defensive tactics, and exploits in the present war ... containing 21 illustrations, etc.*, Whittaker & Co: London, 1915
Domville-Fife, C, *Submarine Warfare of Today*, Seeley, Service & Co: London, 1919
Earle, R, ed., *United States Navy Ordnance Activities, World War I, 1917–18*, Government Printing Office: Washington, DC, 1920
Edwards, K, *We Dive at Dawn*, Rich & Cowan: London, 1939
Gibson, R H and Prendergast, M, *The German Submarine War, 1914–1918*, Constable: London, 1931
Hackmann, W D, *Seek and Strike*, HMSO/Science Museum: London, 1984
Hartmann, G K, *Weapons that Wait*, Naval Institute Press: Washington, DC, 1979
'A History of the Naval Ordnance Inspectorate' by W Stillgate, 1951 [unpublished: copy at Explosion! The Museum of Naval Firepower]
Hutchinson, R, *Beneath the Waves*, Jane's Submarines, 2001
Ingham, A, 'British naval mines and minelayers', unpublished: Priddy's Hard Ordnance Museum, 1981 [held in Museum of Naval Firepower archive]
Jellicoe of Scapa, Viscount, *The Crisis of the Naval War*, Cassell: London, 1920
Knocker, Clinker, *Aye, Aye, Sir*, Rich & Cowan: London, 1938

'List of German submarines sunk on operations during World War One', revd Sep. 1987 [unpublished: document in Royal Navy Submarine Archive]

Messimer, D R, *Find and Destroy*, Naval Institute Press, Annapolis, Maryland, 2001

Navy Records Society, *Anglo-American Naval Relations, 1917–19*, Navy Records Society, Scolar Press: Aldershot, Hants., 1991

Padfield, P, *Aim Straight*, Hodder & Stoughton: London, 1966

Poland, E N, *The Torpedomen: HMS Vernon's Story, 1872–1986* [privately published], K. Mason, Gosport, Hants., 1993

Price, A, *Aircraft versus Submarine: The evolution of the anti-submarine aircraft, 1912 to 1980*, London: Jane's Publishing, 1980

Roskill, S W, *Official History of the Second World War: The war at sea, 1939–45*, London: HMSO, 1954

Sayer, G B, *HMS Vernon*, Wardroom Mess Committee, HMS *Vernon*

Sims, William S, *The Victory at Sea*, Doubleday Page & Co: Garden City, New York, 1920

Taprell Dorling, Henry ['Taffrail'], *Swept Channels*, Hodder & Stoughton: London, 1935

Webb, E D, *HMS Vernon: a short history from 1930–1955*, Wardroom Mess Committee, HMS *Vernon*

Williams, Mark, *Captain Gilbert Roberts, R.N., and the Anti-U-boat School*, London: Cassell, 1979

Wadlow, E C, 'Mechanical engineering aspects of naval mining', *Proceedings of the Institute of Mechanical Engineers*, February 1948

Notes

Chapter One

1 Hackmann, *Seek and Strike*, p. 9.
2 Ibid.
3 Bennett, *Naval Battles of the First World War*, p. 260.
4 Navy Records Society, *Anglo-American Naval Relations, 1917–19* (1991), p. 223.
5 'List of German submarines sunk on operations during World War One', Royal Navy Submarine Archive document (revd September 1987), p. 1.
6 The gun had a 3in barrel, which weighed 20cwt (1 ton). This nomenclature came into use in the Victorian period to distinguish different types of gun of the same calibre.
7 Hutchinson, *Beneath the Waves*, p. 68.
8 Cope-Cornford, *Paravane Adventure*, p. 46.
9 This figure comes from Hutchinson, *Beneath the Waves*; 'List of German submarines sunk on operations during World War One', pp. 1–11, says fifty-five were lost.
10 Annual Report of the Torpedo School, HMS *Vernon* (1915), p. 162.
11 Depth Charge Pocket Book, Torpedo and Mining Dept, BR 1063, 1944, p. 3.

Chapter Two

1 Taylor papers, Explosion: Museum of Naval Firepower.
2 Ibid.
3 Ross, J, *The Years of My Pilgrimage*, Arnold: London, 1924.
4 Walter Conan, as quoted in *Blackrock Magazine*.
5 NA ADM 199/1175, Enclosure II.
6 Sims, *Victory at Sea*, p. 94.
7 Ibid.
8 ADM 199/1175, Enclosure II.
9 NA TS32/87.
10 Jellicoe, *Crisis of the Naval War*, p. 57.

Chapter Three

1 Captain Martin Fielding, RNR, quoted in Taprell Dorling, *Swept Channels*.
2 *Jane's Fighting Ships*, Jane's Publications: London, 1919, pp. 85–90.
3 Navy Records Society, *Anglo-American Naval Relations*, p. 292.
4 Annual Report of the Torpedo School, HMS *Vernon*, 1915, plate 73.
5 NA T173/464.
6 Annual Report of the Torpedo School, HMS *Vernon*, 1913, pp. 70–71.
7 Ibid., p. 174.
8 Cope-Cornford, *Paravane Adventure*, p. 27.
9 Taprell Dorling, *Swept Channels*, p. 117.
10 See *Aim Straight* by Peter Padfield, who seems to imply that the Admiralty developed Scott's idea and this was clearly not the case: p. 231.
11 NA TS 32/87, Gwynne's deposition.
12 NA TS 32/87, Q.41.
13 ADM 189/99.
14 Ibid.
15 NA T173/464, Form 3.
16 Letter under ref. G.O.2658.17.20355: Museum of Naval Firepower, Gosport, inscription found upon presentation plate of Mark II thrower, held as a presentation piece at Vosper Thornycroft, Woolston.
17 ADM 1/8552/59.
18 NA T1/12242 48389/18.

Chapter Four

1 Director of Underwater Weapons, 'Technical history of anti-submarine weapons', p. 41.
2 Hackmann, *Seek and Strike*, p. 9.
3 NA TS32/87.
4 Jellicoe, *Crisis of the Naval War*
5 BR 1063, pp. 11–12.
6 Deposition of commanding officer HM Submarine J2, typed at HMS *Titania*, September 1917, Royal Navy Submarine Museum archive.
7 Royal Navy Submarine Museum archive, document A2000/363.
8 Edwards, *We Dive at Dawn*, p. 364.
9 Jellicoe, *Crisis of the Naval War*, p. 51.
10 Memo from Superintendent Armament Supply Officer on Priddy's Hard during the First World War, 30 January 1919. Explosion: Museum of Naval Firepower archive.
11 Ibid.
12 Ibid.
13 Ibid.
14 Messimer, *Find and Destroy*, pp. 223–4.

15 Navy Records Society, *Anglo-American Naval Relations*, p. 301.

16 Most of the information on hydrophones comes from Hackmann, with reference to the Torpedo School annual report.

Chapter Five

1 Clinker Knocker, *Aye, Aye, Sir*, p. 227. This curious book was supposedly written by a stoker in the First World War but was probably written by a junior officer. It deals with life at sea, but clearly draws on experiences of P-boats in the war.

2 Capt. Martin Fielding, RNR, in Taprell Dorling, *Swept Channels*, pp. 228–9.

3 Jellicoe, *Crisis of the Naval War*

4 Ibid., p. 90.

5 Ibid., p. 77.

6 Poland, *The Torpedomen*, p. 70.

7 Taprell Dorling, *Swept Channels*, p. 29.

8 Cope-Cornford, *Paravane Adventure*, p. 71.

9 Ibid., pp. 246–7.

10 Ingham, *British Naval Mines and Minelayers*

11 ADM 199/1175, case 7.

12 Cowie, *Mines, Minelayers and Minesweeping*, p. 44.

13 Hartmann, *Weapons that Wait*, p. 238.

Chapter Six

1 NA ADM 186/376, pp. 2–4.

2 Messimer, *Find and Destroy*, p. 222.

3 Ibid.

4 Annual Report of the Torpedo School, HMS *Vernon*, 1915, p. 155.

5 Taprell Dorling, *Swept Channels*, p. 125.

6 Campbell, *Naval Weapons of World War Two*, p. 269.

7 Poland, *The Torpedomen*, pp. 182–3. The nomenclature used by naval establishments is confusing, since earlier references in the annual reports of the Torpedo School at HMS *Vernon* normally refer to German mines by roman numerals, but evaluations in the Second World War name them alphabetically.

8 Brennecke, *Hunter and Hunted*, p. 38.

9 TR/P1/2437/ND, manufacturing leaflet by Pignone, p. 2.

Chapter Seven

1 Earle, *United States Navy Ordnance Activities, World War I, 1917–18*, p. 98.

2 NA TS 32/87.

3 Navy Records Society, *Anglo-American Naval Relations*, p. 219.

4 Jellicoe, *Crisis of the Naval War*, p. 181.

5 NA TS 32/87.
6 Ibid.
7 Earle, *United States Navy Ordnance Activities, World War I, 1917–18*, p. 99.
8 NA TS 32/87.
9 Taylor MSS, Museum of Naval Firepower, Commission for the Adjustment of British Claims [pamphlet], p. 20.
10 NA TS 32/87.
11 Hartmann, *Weapons that Wait*, p. 51.
12 Taylor MSS, Museum of Naval Firepower, Before the Commission for the Adjustment of British Claims, Cornelius Ford, Washington DC, 1931–2 [pamphlet], p. 23.
13 Taylor MSS, Museum of Naval Firepower, Commission for the Adjustment of British Claims [pamphlet], p. 27.
14 Taylor MSS, Museum of Naval Firepower, letter from Vickers-Armstrong, Barrow-in-Furness, 23 January 1967.

Chapter Eight
1 Superintendent of Mine Design, August 1936.
2 Pierse report, archive document held in the Museum of Naval Firepower, Gosport.
3 There are endless discussions about the origin of the term 'ASDIC' – for one of the best descriptions, see Hackmann, *Seek and Strike*, p. xxv.
4 Poland, *The Torpedomen*, p. 248.
5 NA ADM 199/1175.
6 Letter from Alan Pilledge to Chris Henry, 11 October 2004, p. 2.
7 ADM 1/13941, letter to Director of Torpedoes and Mines.
8 ADM 137/3261.

Chapter Nine
1 Wood, quoted in Hartmann, *Weapons that Wait*, p. 62.
2 Letter from Alan Pilledge to Chris Henry, 11 October 2004.
3 Letter from Alan Pilledge to Chris Henry, 25 August 2003.
4 Letter from Alan Pilledge to Chris Henry, 11 October 2004.
5 Wadlow, E, 'Wartime memories of Leigh Park House', *Hampshire Magazine* (February 1987), pp. 49–50.
6 Letter from Alan Pilledge to Chris Henry, October 2004, p. 2.
7 Poland, *The Torpedomen*, p. 219.
8 Director of Underwater Weapons, 'Technical history of anti-submarine weapons', p. 2.
9 ADM 253/790, p. 16.
10 Busch, *U-boats at War*, pp. 55–6.
11 Ibid.

12 Buchheim, *U-boat War*, p. 110.
13 Beevor, *Crete: the Battle and the Resistance*, p. 161. It should be emphasized that this was a rumour, but one which the author has heard of before in other theatres.

Chapter Ten

1 Director of Underwater Weapons, 'Technical history of anti-submarine weapons', pp. 8–9.
2 Hackmann, *Seek and Strike*, p. 308.
3 Director of Underwater Weapons, 'Technical history of anti-submarine weapons', p. 131.
4 Ibid., p. 152.
5. ADM 253/790.
6. ADM 116/5246, pp. 1–5.
7. WO 198/8464, pp. 1–2.

Chapter Eleven

1. Comments from Captain (S), 12th Submarine Flotilla, Trials of X-craft side charges, Box ADM 1/14811, doc. NA MAF 131/155.
2. Personal recollections of David Clark, December 2004.
3. Letter from Alan Pilledge to Chris Henry, 11 October 2004.
4. Comments from Captain (S), 12th Submarine Flotilla, Trials of X-craft side charges, NA MAF 131/155.
5. Letter in Royal Navy Submarine Archive, document 1942/009.
6. Ibid., letter from captains, 5th Submarine Flotilla, to Admiral Submarines, 1 July 1942, p. 1.

Chapter Twelve

1. Wadlow, 'Mechanical engineering aspects of naval mining', p. 12.
2. Alan Pilledge, personal communication to the author.

Index